LOCOMOTION PAPERS   LP191

The
Lampeter, Aberayron
and
New Quay
Light Railway

by
M.R.C. Price

THE OAKWOOD PRESS

© Oakwood Press and M.R.C. Price, 2011

British Library Cataloguing in Publication Data
A Record for this book is available from the British Library
ISBN 978 0 85361 714 3

First Published 1995
Second Edition 2011

Typeset by Oakwood Graphics.
Repro by PKmediaworks, Cranborne, Dorset.
Printed by Information Press Ltd, Eynsham, Oxford.

All rights reserved. No part of this book may be reproduced or transmitted in any form or by any means, electronic or mechanical, including photocopying, recording or by any information storage and retrieval system, without permission from the Publisher in writing.

Dedication

For Roger, in sincere appreciation for many hours of advice and guidance in the art of railway history, always willingly given.

Above: A postcard view of Aberayron harbour c. 1910.   *Author's Collection*

Title Page: The seal of the Lampeter, Aberayron & New Quay Light Railway.
The GWR Museum, Swindon, and Thamesdown Borough Council

Front cover: Ex-GWR 0-6-0PT No. 7407 stands in the platform at Aberayron with the branch goods train in September 1960.   *J.I.C. Boyd*
Rear cover, top: A view looking towards Lampeter of Ciliau Aeron station from the brake van of the branch goods train on 7th July, 1958.   *H.C. Casserley*
Rear cover, bottom: A Railway Clearing House map showing the Aberayron branch and the proposed line to New Quay.   *Oakwood Collection*

Published by The Oakwood Press (Usk), P.O. Box 13, Usk, Mon., NP15 1YS.
E-mail: sales@oakwoodpress.co.uk
Website: www.oakwoodpress.co.uk

Contents

	Introduction	5
Chapter One	Early Schemes	7
Chapter Two	The Lampeter Route	13
Chapter Three	Building the Line	21
Chapter Four	The Heyday of the Railway	37
Chapter Five	Under the Great Western	43
Chapter Six	Decline and Fall	51
Chapter Seven	Locomotives and Rolling Stock	61
Chapter Eight	The Route Described	67
Chapter Nine	Postscript	87
Appendix One	The New Quay Harbour Tramway	93
Appendix Two	Extracts from the Lampeter Aberayron and New Quay Light Railway Order 1906	96
Appendix Three	Board of Trade Inspector's Report, 1911	98
Appendix Four	LA&NQLR Chairman's Report, 1913	100
Appendix Five	LA&NQLR Chairman's Report, 1922	101
Appendix Six	Appendix to the Working Timetable, 1939	102
	Bibliography	104
	Acknowledgements	104

This image was captioned 'One of the GWR auto-cars to run on the new Lampeter-Aberayron railway' when first published. *GWR Publicity Department, 1911*

Aberayron Harbour c. 1925. Spillers & Bakers Ltd, later Spillers Ltd, shipped flour from Cardiff to Aberayron from 1921 to 1934, providing the harbour with some of its last commercial traffic. After this coastal traffic ended, flour was transported to Aberayron by rail.
Author's Collection

A tinted postcard view of New Quay, c. 1910. The quarry which provided stone for the harbour is out of view to the left; the terminus of the intended New Quay branch of the LA&NQLR would have been near the houses on the extreme right. *Author's Collection*

Introduction

For a small book this has had an inordinately long period of gestation. My first encounter with the line was in the early 1960s, when steam was still king, there were wagons in the sidings at Aberayron, and weeds covered the platforms of the wayside halts. The passage of the daily goods train was part of an agreeable, and seemingly settled way of life. Although in London Dr Beeching was sharpening his axe, on a Spring morning in Cardiganshire it was as hard to contemplate the destruction of the railway, as it might ever be to imagine the death of a friend.

The good intention to go more deeply into the Aberayron story, and enlarge early notes, has been deferred many times. In 1987, however, The Oakwood Press prompted me to take action, and visits were duly made to the Public Record Office and the National Library of Wales, as well as the Aberayron district. My hope now is that this account will convey something of the character of this beautiful Welsh by-way. Under the Great Western it became the kind of branch which was that company's speciality - from Kington to Kingsbridge, and from Cleobury Mortimer to Cardigan. Considering the affection so many modellers and artists feel for the Great Western's country branches, the Aberayron line might well be a candidate for their attention. I am not aware that it has ever been so, but maybe that will change. At all events, I must express my sincere thanks to the many people who have helped in this endeavour, and not least the present and past proprietors of the Oakwood Press, Jane Kennedy and Roger Kidner. As Roger has been resident for some time in the Cardiganshire part of Dyfed, it seems entirely appropriate that this piece of work should be dedicated to him. A full list of acknowledgements is provided on another page, but special thanks are due to John de Havilland for his splendid maps, and to my family for allowing me the space to undertake both the research and the writing.

Martin Connop Price
Shiplake, Oxfordshire
August 1994

N.B. In this book the spelling 'Aberayron' is preferred to the Welsh 'Aberaeron', because the former spelling was always favoured for railway purposes. Welsh place names were often anglicized by railway companies based in England.

Between 1886 and 1931 an aerial ropeway operated across Aberayron Harbour from Quay Parade on the north side and Belle Vue Terrace on the south. Latterly a four-seater carriage was used, carrying the title 'Aeron Express'; at the turn of the century - as this postcard view shows - a two-seater carriage was employed. *Author's Collection*

A view of the horse drawn mail and passenger van which was used between Aberayron and Lampeter before the construction of the railway. *B. Hilton Collection*

Chapter One

Early Schemes

The small town of Aberayron lies about 16 miles south of Aberystwyth on the wide sweep of Cardigan Bay. Until the start of the 19th century it was little more than a cluster of cottages near the mouth of the small Aeron river, in the parish of Henfynyw. Such coastal trade as existed passed mostly through the tiny port of Llandewi Aberarth, about two miles to the north. However, early in the century it was Aberayron which was transformed by the enterprise of the Revd Alban Jones Gwynne. In 1805 he had the fortune to inherit over £100,000, and following the passing of an Act of Parliament in 1807 he began to apply his money for the construction of harbour quays and associated buildings. His plan was to develop Aberayron as a focus for Cardiganshire trade, and this was assisted by the granting of 99 year leases to builders who were ready to conform with an overall town planning scheme. The result was a 'new town', notable for its dignity, order and space, adjoining a well protected harbour, completed in 1811. Unfortunately Gwynne died only a few years later in 1819, but his efforts were duly recognized by naming part of the centre of the town Alban Square.

Alban Gwynne did not confine his attention to Aberayron, because shortly before his death he asked the well-known engineer John Rennie to carry out a survey of the bay at New Quay, a small port five miles south of Aberayron. Rennie's plans and estimates for a new pier at New Quay were deemed too expensive, and nothing was done until 1833, when a company was proposed to build a new harbour at New Quay. Construction began in 1835, and the work included the provision of a railway or tramway to take stone to the harbour works. This very short-lived line, described further in *Appendix One*, appears to have been the first of any kind in southern Cardiganshire.

For many years most of Aberayron's trade was conducted by sea, and the port became busy with traffic in limestone, coal, slate, timber and grain. Although the Act of 1807 gave merchants from Aberarth protection from paying Aberayron harbour dues, their port declined whilst Aberayron prospered. In 1850 local businessmen formed the Aberayron & Bristol Navigation Co., to provide a shipping service to and from Bristol with two small sailing vessels. In September 1863 local initiative went further, with the formation of the Aberayron Steam Navigation Co. Ltd. From 1864 to 1876 this concern operated a service to Bristol using a small steamer named the *Prince Cadwgan*. Although this venture had some limited financial success, it suffered from a lack of goods (apart from grain) for outward shipment. In 1876 the *Prince Cadwgan* was sunk, but by then other shipping companies were ready to visit Aberayron. In the 1880s a large traffic in pigs developed, and in one 12 month period the vessel *Ianthe* actually shipped 25,000 pigs from Aberayron.

In the 19th century Aberayron's hinterland was almost entirely agricultural in character. There were a number of landed estates in the quiet Aeron valley, but these were owned by gentry rather than aristocracy, and the culture was largely rooted in the Welsh language. Some 13 miles south-east of Aberayron lay the pleasant market town of Lampeter, a sizeable settlement by Cardiganshire standards, but with a population of no more than 2,000. In 1822 the foundation stone was laid for St David's College, Lampeter, on a site given by a prominent local landowner, John Scandrett Harford. The College opened its doors to its first students on St David's Day, 1st March, 1827, and very soon developed a considerable reputation for teaching divinity and the arts. For many years this rather remote seat of learning possessed a somewhat unexpected status by virtue of being affiliated to both Oxford and Cambridge Universities. Quite naturally the College came to be regarded with respect and some pride by the residents of Lampeter and district.

The first proposal for a railway to Lampeter and Aberayron appears to have been produced by the well-known Welsh railway contractor, David Davies of Llandinam. In his later years Davies became a local MP, but even as early as 1860 his political aspirations encouraged him to advocate a railway from Pencader on the Carmarthen & Cardigan Railway (C&CR) to Aberayron, by way of Lampeter and the Aeron valley. Although notionally independent, it is believed that this project had the active support of the impecunious C&CR. It failed to make progress for want of finance.

At the time an alternative scheme was well in hand. Ever since the 'Railway Mania' of 1845 there had been persistent hopes for the creation of a direct railway between the cotton and manufacturing districts around Manchester and the deep water port of Milford Haven. It was widely supposed at this period that the increasing trade with North America might lead to the huge natural harbour of Milford Haven surpassing Liverpool in importance. For 15 years nothing came of the Manchester & Milford dream. In 1860, however, an Act was passed approving the building of the Manchester & Milford Railway (M&MR) not between the two places named, but between Llanidloes in mid-Wales and Pencader on the C&CR, to provide a link between other railways already authorized. Given the mountainous terrain of mid-Wales the construction of this line was never going to be easy, and the resources of the M&MR were always limited. The scheme envisaged the railway making a steep climb from Llanidloes to Llangurig and the Wye valley before passing through a tunnel of over a mile to the Rheidol valley above Devil's Bridge. The route then turned south to cross the Ystwyth valley on a viaduct 240 ft high before entering another tunnel and dropping down to the village of Pontrhydfendigaid. From this point the land was more favourable, and easier gradients were anticipated as the line followed the Teifi valley past Tregaron, Lampeter and Llanybyther to Pencader.

Not surprisingly, the M&MR was soon in difficulties. The assumption that industrialists and merchants from Manchester would wish to subscribe capital was found to be mistaken, and in one of the poorer parts of Wales there were relatively few people willing or able to take shares in the company. After a struggle to find finance, a contract was let in 1861 for the building of the first portion of the line, from Llanidloes to Llangurig. The company was not assisted either by rivalries with other railways, or its own turbulent internal politics. The complexities of this period have been described in detail in *The Manchester & Milford Railway* by John Holden (published by The Oakwood Press); suffice to say that the line to Llangurig was completed in 1864, but was not opened to regular traffic. By then the magnitude of the task involved in taking the railway over the mountains was entirely obvious. After much debate about alternative, cheaper routes the company went to Parliament in 1865 for an Act to permit them to build a branch north-west from the proposed main line at Strata Florida to the town of Aberystwyth, where a connection was envisaged with the separate Aberystwyth & Welsh Coast Railway. The southern section from the C&CR at Pencader running up the Teifi valley to Lampeter was opened on 1st June, 1866, and it was soon followed by the section north to Strata Florida on 1st September, 1866. The branch from Strata Florida to Aberystwyth was ready for traffic by 12th August, 1867, but the main line north from Strata Florida to Llangurig proved to be too much for the under funded M&MR, and it was never built.

The history of the C&CR was arguably even more chequered than that of the M&MR. After all manner of problems the line had reached the Teifi valley at Llandyssul, some three miles north-west of Pencader, in June 1864. There it stayed for over 30 years, and travellers for Cardigan had to change at Llandyssul into a horse-drawn omnibus. Before long there was a similar omnibus service from Llandyssul to New Quay on the Cardiganshire coast, but a suggestion that for a time there was also another omnibus service direct to Aberayron is not yet supported by any documentary evidence. Suffice to say that the independent career of the C&CR came to an end in 1881 when the company was taken over by the Great Western Railway (GWR). In the same year Parliamentary powers were obtained for an extension of the line to Newcastle Emlyn, but as the GWR was in no hurry to proceed with the work the extension was not complete and open for traffic until 1st July, 1895. Aberayron is known to have had a horse 'bus service to Aberystwyth by 1875, and very probably earlier. By 1881 it is believed there was also a similar service between New Quay, Aberayron and Aberystwyth. In 1876, however, David Davies (now MP for the Cardiganshire Boroughs) proposed that a railway be built from Llanilar on the M&MR to Llanrhystyd along the valley of the Wyre, before following the coastline of Cardigan Bay down to Aberayron. Davies commitment to this proposal was quite considerable, because he invited the district to find £15,000 towards the cost, and offered to put up another £15,000 himself. Mr Alban Gwynne, a descendant of Revd Alban Jones Gwynne, is said to have responded by subscribing £5,000, but other local residents seem to have been less supportive. At all events, although the project was under discussion for several years, the opportunity was allowed to pass, and the idea appears to have been abandoned in 1880.

In or about 1885 another scheme was put forward, this time for a 2 ft gauge railway approaching from the south. In this instance a certain Stephen Evans and his associates asked J.W. Szlumper to survey a route between Llandyssul on the C&CR and the small port of New Quay. By this time Szlumper had become well known in Cardiganshire for his work on both the M&MR and the Whitland & Cardigan Railway, which had just been built over the Prescelli hills to the county town, and which opened for public traffic on 1st September, 1886. Although the survey was made, the railway was not - for the very familiar reason of shortage of capital. Very soon after the opening of the railway to

10 THE LAMPETER, ABERAYRON AND NEW QUAY LIGHT RAILWAY

Newcastle Emlyn in 1895 the Bishop of Chester wrote to *The Times* urging the construction of the line to New Quay, but from Newcastle Emlyn rather than Llandyssul. Nothing came of his suggestion.

The year 1895 was notable for another reason. A Light Railways conference was held in London to consider possible ways of enabling railways to be built more cheaply for the benefit of rural areas. Wales was well represented, those present including J.M. Howell, chairman of Cardiganshire County Council, and Col H. Davies-Evans, the Lord Lieutenant. John Charles Harford of Falcondale, Lampeter, who had failed to win Cardiganshire for the Conservatives at the 1895 General Election, also attended. He spoke strongly in favour of constructing light railways in his county, and he had the support of others, including Sir Martin Lloyd, who declared that no county in Wales needed light railways more than Cardiganshire. As a result of this important meeting legislation was prepared which was embodied in the Light Railways Act, 1896.

One of the first projects to take advantage of the new legislation was the Vale of Rheidol Light Railway Company. This concern was incorporated by Act of Parliament on 6th August, 1897, to build a narrow gauge railway from Aberystwyth inland up the valley of the Rheidol to Devil's Bridge. Even before the company had obtained these powers, it was proposed that the line should be extended south from Aberystwyth to Aberayron. Although Aberayron was not mentioned in the 1897 Act, it was realised that the extension might be built as a light railway. Accordingly the idea was referred to at a meeting of the Light Railway Commissioners held at Aberystwyth in April 1898, and it was noted that the extension would provide small, but stone-built stations at several villages - including Llanychaiarn, Llanddeinol and Llanrhystyd. On 13th August, 1898, the Vale of Rheidol obtained a Light Railway Order to construct a railway of 2 ft gauge for 16 miles 3 furlongs from Aberystwyth to Aberayron in the parish of Llandewi-Aberarth. Although provision was made for some slight variations in gauge and alignment, it was stipulated that the line should be completed within three years. Axle-loadings were restricted to 9 tons per axle, and a speed limit of 17 mph was specified. One of the more interesting aspects of the Light Railway Order was its provision for other forms of motive power besides steam, including electricity. The company was empowered to increase its capital by £25,000 ordinary shares, £38,000 preference shares, and £21,000 in debentures. It was made very clear, however, that extension capital should be kept apart from that raised for the original line, and that the two undertakings had to be treated as quite separate and distinct. Two years later, in recognition that costs were rising, a second Act of Parliament allowed the Vale of Rheidol to increase its share capital by £12,000, and its borrowing powers by £4,000.

The Aberayron extension had the backing of the Cardiganshire County Council, and other public authorities, but encountered the hostility of the Manchester & Milford Railway, which regarded Aberayron as being within its area. While the promoters considered this difficulty, they decided to press ahead with the building of the line up the Rheidol Valley. In January 1901, a contract for the construction of this route was granted to Pethick Bros, of Plymouth, who had worked with the engineer, J.W. Szlumper, on the building of the Lynton & Barnstaple Railway in North Devon. Construction costs on the

EARLY SCHEMES 11

principal undertaking amounted to about £3,250 per mile, and the railway to Devil's Bridge was eventually opened to goods traffic in August 1902, and to passengers from 5th November, 1902.

By this time it was clear that the Aberayron extension would be a more expensive undertaking, and it had been estimated that the costs would amount to £3,850 per mile. On 1st August, 1902, the Board of Trade granted another Light Railway Order, the main feature of which was an extension of time for the completion of the extension to 12th August, 1905, with land acquisition to be completed a year earlier. The Order also contained provisions easing construction costs by dispensing with several bridges over roads on the Aberayron extension, and relieving the company of responsibility for maintaining diverted roads after just one year. No doubt in recognition of the County Council's support, the Order authorized the Council to lend up to £18,000 towards the extension project.

Messrs Pethick took shares instead of cash for much of their work on the Vale of Rheidol, and so gained an increasing stake in the company. By 1903 they had completed work on the Devil's Bridge line, and had every reason to be interested in new contracts. On 26th February, 1903, there were three members of the Pethick family on the Vale of Rheidol Board, and no less than eight Pethicks amongst the shareholders. There can be little doubt that their influence was decisive in persuading the Directors on the same day to renew their commitment to make the Aberayron extension; as evidence of the Board's good intentions four of their number were asked to form an independent Aberayron Extension Committee. Mr A.H. Pethick soon offered to put up £10,000 of the capital required, and in May 1903 the County Council agreed to provide the £18,000 authorized for the venture, on the basis that the company find the other sums necessary within six months. For a while hopes were high, but once again the company found it difficult to attract significant financial backing from other sources.

Under the 1902 Light Railway Order land acquisition had to be completed by 12th August, 1904, but by the beginning of the year very little had been achieved. In February the Chairman of the Vale of Rheidol, Mr Montague Smith, resigned on grounds of ill-health. He was replaced by A.H. Pethick, who was becoming increasingly frustrated by the delays and difficulties confronting the company. In July 1904, it was suggested that powers be obtained to enable the extension to be built to the standard gauge, with the Cambrian Railways then being invited to work the line. The supposed advantage of this proposal was that the standard gauge junction could be 3 miles south of Aberystwyth, near Llanrhystyd Road on the M&MR, a point significantly closer to Aberayron. Although A.H. Pethick was sympathetic to this idea, it did not ease his immediate worries. Early in August 1904, the Board admitted to the County Council that the money for the extension could not be found - and this was for the narrow gauge scheme! Gloom descended upon the Aberayron Extension Committee: it was not lifted greatly when, in November 1904, the Cambrian Railways declared that a line south from Llanrhystyd Road to New Quay could be built for £180,000, including rolling stock. Although this pleased some notable New Quay residents, nothing was done, and eventually the idea was abandoned.

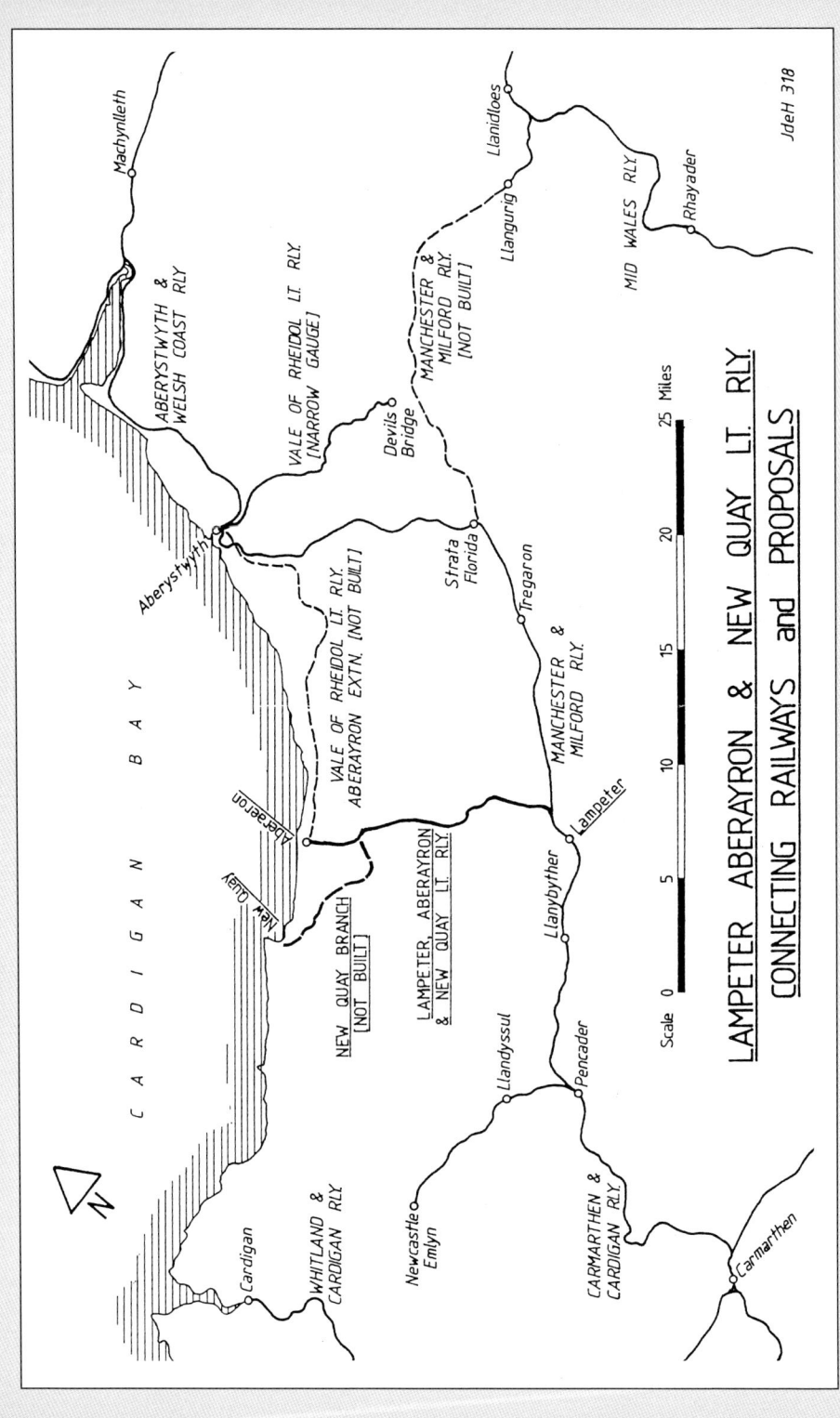

Chapter Two

The Lampeter Route

In 1903 there was genuine difference of opinion as to the best way to bring a railway to Aberayron. Some favoured the Vale of Rheidol's route from the north; others believed it would be better to build up the Aeron valley from the south. By now efforts were being made to promote a standard gauge railway from Llandilo to Aberayron, or from Lampeter to Aberayron. This initiative came largely from local landowners, and although the scheme was advanced in two sections (Llandilo-Lampeter, and Lampeter-Aberayron) the same engineers, Messrs S.W. and A.L. Yockney of Westminster, were employed to draw up the plans and sections for both. The leading promoters of the Llandilo & Lampeter line were Sir James Hamlyn Williams-Drummond Bt, Lt Gen. Sir James Hill-Johnes, and John Morgan Davies; the leading figures behind the Lampeter & Aberayron line were John Charles Harford, Col Herbert Davies-Evans, Major Price Lewes and Capt. Herbert Vaughan. In June 1903, the Mayor of Lampeter, Prof. Walker of St David's College, called for the construction of both sections, and indeed initially both advanced in tandem.

These proposals not only offered a solution to the old question of how best to serve Aberayron by rail, but with the Llandilo and Lampeter line also offered the possibility of a much more direct route between Cardiganshire and the well populated areas of South Wales. Regrettably, but understandably the impecunious Manchester & Milford Railway regarded the Llandilo and Lampeter scheme as a threat to its own income, and so objected at every turn. In contrast it co-operated with the Lampeter & Aberayron (L&A) project, perceiving that this offered the possibility of some additional traffic. Against this background it was soon decided that the two lines should be promoted separately, and be entirely distinct.

It appears that Mr S.W. Yockney conducted a preliminary survey of the Lampeter-Aberayron route before the end of 1903. When the Light Railway Commissioners held an inquiry at Lampeter on 26th January, 1904, he was able to provide an estimate that the works and land would cost £88,000. In addition it was estimated that rolling stock would cost £10,000 and administrative costs, including the obtaining of a Light Railway Order, would cost £11,723. By March 1904, the Engineer had refined the figure for the total cost of land and works to £88,277, and he expected the building of the railway to cost an average of £5,852 per mile. Stations on the line were proposed at Silian, Blaenplwyf, Talsarn Road, Ystrad, Neuadd-ddu, New Inn (Llanerch Ayron) and Aberayron. According to the deposited plans it was envisaged at this stage that the new railway would have its own station at Lampeter, just west of the M&MR station, and it appears that this was also intended to be used by services on the Llandilo-Lampeter line. Even so, the Engineer recognised that a considerable saving could be achieved if traffic on the proposed new lines could be routed into the M&MR station. Meanwhile the M&M Directors were less than amused to learn that the promoters of the Aberayron line were seeking general powers to make

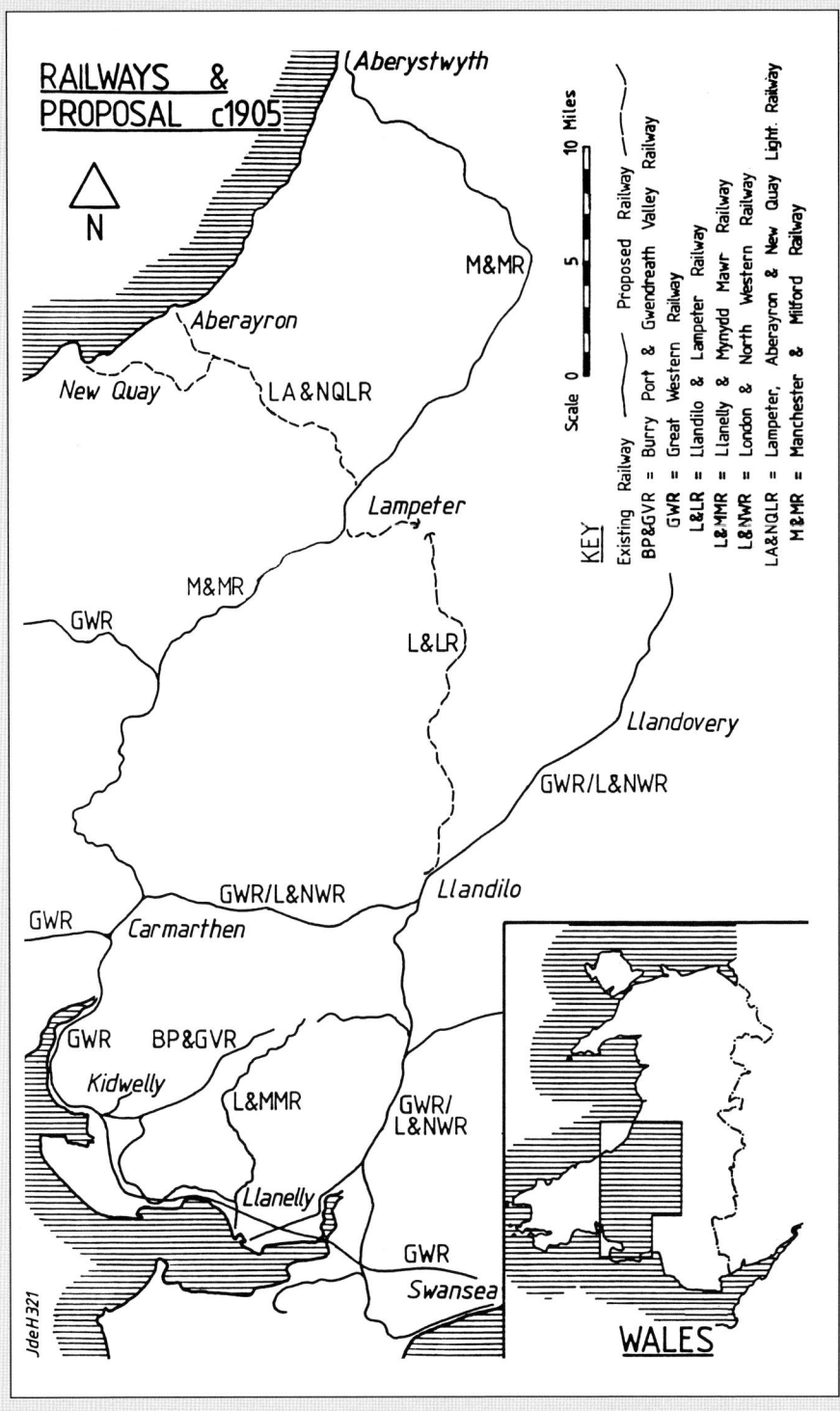

working agreements with other railways, rather than exclusive powers with the M&M. At this stage the Manchester & Milford were offering to work the new line at cost, together with 25 per cent of the profits. An optimistic bid by the L&A to obtain a minimum guaranteed profit agreement was firmly resisted.

During 1904 Messrs Yockney were working on the Llandilo and Lampeter scheme as well as on the Aberayron line, and by May 1905, they had prepared a case for the Light Railway Commissioners. This described the Llandilo and Lampeter route in five distinct sections, of which railway No. 1 (from Llandilo to Llancrwys) was 15¾ miles long, and railway No. 2 (from Llancrwys almost to Lampeter) was 6 miles long. The total length of all five sections was about 23 miles, and the total cost of land and construction was estimated at £153,853. The district it was intended to serve was no more populated than the Aeron valley north of Lampeter, but the line was designed to pass the small villages of Talley, Llansawel, Pumpsaint (near Dolaucothi) and Farmers (near Llancrwys). Although the Light Railway Commissioners saw the merits of the scheme, it appears that the line was presented primarily as a local branch - perhaps to try to allay the anxieties of the M&MR. Arguably the concept of the line as a significant through route never had much credibility; what is certain is that the venture failed to attract the substantial financial backing it needed.

In rural Cardiganshire it was not easy to raise funds for the Aberayron line, let alone the Llandilo and Lampeter. Whilst the various local authorities in the county expressed great interest in new railways, they met competing claims for their limited resources. In May 1905, the Finance Committee of Cardiganshire County Council heard arguments in favour of both the Lampeter & Aberayron project and also the proposal to build a line from Llanrhystyd Road to New Quay. Mr W.W. Grierson of the M&MR put the case for the Lampeter, Aberayron & New Quay line. He declared that the 21¼ miles of railway (including rolling stock) would cost £150,000, comprising £87,000 for the 13½ miles from Lampeter to Aberayron, and £63,000 for the 7¾ mile branch to New Quay. On the basis that the County Council might put up £30,000, he observed that the Treasury would then be empowered to advance a similar sum, leaving some £90,000 to be raised by the promoters. The directors of the M&MR offered to provide £5,000 on condition that they were allowed to manage the line, and work it for 50 per cent of earnings. It was clearly never going to be a source of riches, because it was estimated that gross receipts would be just £10 per mile per week!

The alternative scheme was presented by residents of New Quay and district, most notably Mr Timothy and Captain Thomas, accompanied by Mr C.S. Denniss, the General Manager of the Cambrian Railways. At this stage the Cambrian was labouring under the illusion that it might soon be able enter into a working agreement with the Manchester & Milford, and on this assumption Mr Denniss pressed the case for the 23 miles of railway from Llanrhystyd Road to New Quay. The cost (including rolling stock) was estimated at £180,000, and again it was hoped that the County Council (and other local bodies) would advance £30,000, and that this sum would be matched by the Treasury. It was anticipated that £50,000 could be raised by the issue of 4½ per cent debentures, and additional sums of £25,000 each through the issue of 5 per cent preference

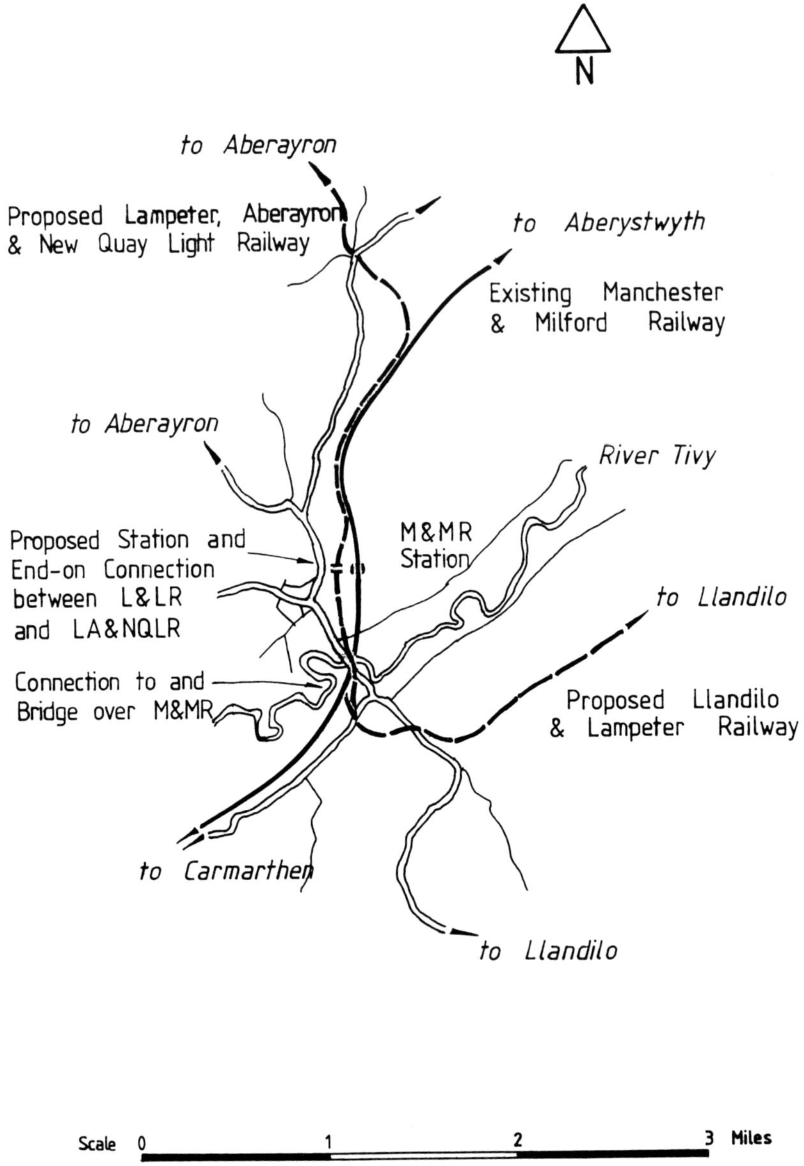

PROPOSALS AT LAMPETER c1905

JdeH 322

stock and ordinary stock. It was supposed that the remaining £20,000 would come from a Treasury free grant.

The Llanrhystyd Road-New Quay line not only involved heavier costs, but also it relied upon the Cambrian having a say in the working of the M&MR. This was not to the liking of the Great Western Railway. From about 1902 the GWR had operated seasonal through coaches and occasional through trains, over the M&MR, and it valued this access to Aberystwyth, not least for tourist traffic. Taking steps to defend its position, the Great Western negotiated its own working agreement with the Manchester & Milford Railway. In July 1905, the GWR sought approval for the agreement from the Court of Chancery, the Cambrian contesting the case on the grounds that it was willing to offer better terms. The eventual outcome was the Manchester & Milford Leasing Act, 1906, whereby the GWR won a lease of the M&MR from 1st July, 1906. The Cambrian gained the somewhat dubious privilege of control of the M&M's isolated and long abandoned Llangurig branch for a rental of £50 per annum. Accordingly it is believed that Great Western trains began running into Aberystwyth from Carmarthen in July 1906. Before long the Cambrian faced direct competition when a through coach from Paddington was included in this service.

As the Llanrhystyd Road to New Quay scheme faded from view, hopes were high for the Lampeter, Aberayron & New Quay (LA&NQ) project. In November 1905, a tender to build both lines was obtained from Messrs Jackson & Co., of London SW1. These contractors were ready to do the work for £139,750, and in addition offered to provide the balance of the required capital by accepting shares in payment. Much encouraged, the railway promoters attended a meeting of Cardiganshire County Council at Lampeter on 8th February, 1906, to seek financial help. Terms for advances of £20,000 and £10,000 were sought from the County Council and local district council respectively, to enable them to secure the equivalent Treasury grant of £30,000. Mr A.L. Yockney attended on behalf of the promoters, a Captain Wilson attended on behalf of Messrs Jackson & Co., and Mr W.W. Grierson on behalf of the M&MR. The continuing support of the latter company was shown by Mr Grierson's statement that the total mileage of the LA&NQ line would be cut to 20 miles, costing an average of almost £7,000 per mile. The anticipated outlay on construction (£139,700) excluded land and rolling stock, the land being likely to cost up to £6,000.

These representations seem to have been well received, but the promoters (who themselves owned sizeable portions of the required land) were becoming impatient. Even before the Treasury had replied to their application for a grant, and long before the issue of the necessary Light Railway Order, they wanted to see building begin. Noting this, Messrs Jackson & Co. wrote to the leading landowner promoter, John Harford, on 27th March, 1906, to say that they would be willing to enter into a provisional arrangement on an assurance from the promoters that they would be paid for work done in accordance with their tender, 'subject to the company obtaining the Treasury grant and the local contributions amounting in the aggregate to £65,000 as contemplated, and the Order confirmed'. In brief nothing could be done until the Light Railway Order was made, and the finances sorted out. Both took longer than the promoters

The three GWR Milnes-Daimler omnibuses parked outside the Feathers Hotel, Aberayron in 1906.

R.W. Kidner Collection

BUILDING THE LINE 23

Fathers'). The only slight flaw in the proceedings was the late arrival of some fireworks, causing a display to be postponed by a couple of days.

With construction now started the Directors could look to the future with more confidence. Already they had given some thought to the means of working the line upon completion. At a Board meeting held on 29th December, 1908, at Falcondale, near Lampeter, the home of J.C. Harford, the Chairman read correspondence on this subject between the company's solicitors and the GWR. Bearing in mind the early interest shown by the Manchester & Milford Railway, it might be supposed that the earliest negotiations would have been with the M&MR. By December 1908, however, the long term independence of that company was clearly in doubt, and a take-over by the GWR was in prospect.

The first of the terms proposed by the GWR to the Aberayron company was that £300 should be retained out of gross annual receipts to cover costs of working and maintenance. Second, they stipulated that the working company should retain 60 per cent of gross receipts provided these amounted to £3,000 per annum, failing which they would be entitled to make up the deficiency from the other 40 per cent. Third and last, if gross receipts should be less than £3,000 in any one year, then for a period of 4 years from the opening of the line to public traffic the GWR would accept such gross receipts, and not carry forward any deficiency against future earnings. The GWR clearly did not have high expectations for the new line's financial prospects; the Directors may have been more optimistic, but they agreed to accept these terms without further debate. In truth they had little choice. The terms were duly embodied in an agreement signed in February 1909.

At the same Board meeting on 29th December, 1908, it was decided to seek Board of Trade consent to certain amendments to the 1906 Light Railway Order. These included the appointment of a County Council representative to the directorate, and alterations to the alignment of the railway at each end of the line. At Aberayron it was proposed to relinquish a small part of the route, and acquire further land to enable the railway to be extended nearer the centre of the town. As regards the southern end, it was decided to seek powers to abandon a portion of the authorized line near Lampeter, and obtain authority to form a re-aligned junction with the M&MR. The proposal for Aberayron proved to be very short-lived, because on 12th January, 1909 it was noted that the Board had entirely abandoned the extension of the line to the Post Office in Aberayron. They were however keen to press on with powers for some changes near Ystrad, for what became known as the 'Brynog deviation'. Somewhat surprisingly the Minutes make no mention of the financial obstacles to the construction of the line to New Quay, even though the Order authorizing its abandonment was granted at this time. Indeed New Quay is hardly mentioned anywhere in the recorded Minutes, suggesting that the very idea of building a line to this village had either gone or was given a low priority.

In the first seven months of 1909 the company Minutes were brief on most topics, and also somewhat predictable in content. Reference was made to the resignation of a Director, Lt A.L. Gwynne, and the appointment in his stead of F.D. Harford, a relative of the Chairman. In the meantime the contractor was working steadily, and required stage payments. Land purchases were still being

Two views of Aberayron station and the end of the line prior to opening.
Lens of Sutton and Ceredigion Museum, Aberystwyth

completed, and the necessary cheques were drawn. In July the valuer, Mr Dudley Drummond, reported that his valuation for the whole of the land required amounted to £6,074 15s. 0d. At the same time a second instalment was paid for the installation of the junction near Lampeter, and a Prospectus for shareholders was issued. One of the more interesting, if inconclusive, pieces of correspondence originated with the Navvy Mission. This worthy Christian body was very probably hoping to appoint a missioner to men on the works, but the Aberayron company appears to have stalled, and no action was taken.

The Prospectus for shareholders was not very successful. When the Directors met at the end of July at their solicitors' offices in Bristol, they were told that applications had been received for 1,423 preference shares, and just 112 ordinary shares. This was regarded as most unsatisfactory, and like so many rural railway companies before them, the LA&NQ Light Railway had to turn to their contractors to help. It was decided that F.D. Harford, together with the Engineer, S.W. Yockney, and the company solicitor should meet the contractor to explain the company's financial difficulties, and ask him to take a further part of the contract in shares. In addition, those who had subscribed were soon receiving calls on their shares, and a mortgage of £2,000 was raised from the Cardiganshire County Council.

The Directors appear to have had some modest success with these measures, but, by September 1909, they were confronted with requests for improvements from the GWR. The Board responded by writing to the Great Western to say that whilst they were 'in a position to carry out the contract entered into with Messrs Nuttall, they do not feel justified in carrying out improvements and additions suggested by the GWR which, though no doubt desirable, are not included in the contract price, and are outside the scope of a light railway'. To use a cricketing analogy, the Great Western's yorker was played with a straight bat. It was also driven towards the boundary, because the Board advised the GWR that it would be willing to meet their suggestions if the GWR would meet the expense. As if to emphasize the point, the Board also resolved to arrange with the GWR for a supply of ballast for Messrs Nuttall 'provided their so doing involves the company in no additional cost'.

Mr Yockney was the centre of attention at a Board meeting held on 16th October, 1909, when he had both good news and bad news to offer. The bad news concerned problems with construction - for example, running sand in a cutting at Glandenys, and water affecting the formation at Blaenplwyf crossing, and on the level between Green Grove and Tanrallt. There was also a land valuation problem at Llanayron, which was settled in November.

The good news was provided by the Engineer producing plans of Aberayron and Ystrad stations, and also the halts at Ciliau, Talsarn and Silian. These were studied with considerable interest, and although approved subject to the GWR's views, they gave rise to much discussion in this and subsequent meetings. At Aberayron it was felt that the sidings were cramped, and that the river bridge on the approach to the station should be widened, and two lines provided instead of the one agreed in the contract. The additional cost was estimated at £577. At Ystrad it was proposed that a siding be made three chains longer than previously stipulated, and at Talsarn it was suggested that a siding should be

Great Western 0-4-2T No. 840 at Aberayron with inspection saloon No. 6477. This vehicle was an ex-Bristol & Exeter Railway carriage. The photograph is believed to have been taken in 1911, prior to the opening of the line.
National Library of Wales

situated to the east of the public road. In the meantime, the suggestion of the GWR's Engineer for supply of its permanent way materials was accepted, and it was agreed that the Aberayron company should obtain 10,000 cu. yards of bottom ballast at a cost not exceeding £100.

Almost a month later, on 11th November, Mr Yockney was able to tell the Board that 3½ miles of permanent way had been laid, and that the GWR Engineer had applied for £350 in respect of the sum of £1,750 agreed for chaired track and permanent way materials. It was duly decided to issue the necessary cheque. The company's Engineer also advised that Great Western proposals for easing certain curves would cost £500. Predictably the Directors felt that this expense should be met by the GWR itself, although within a month the company was allowing £88 for alterations to a curve at Penwern, near Ystrad. After further discussion about Talsarn, it was now resolved that the halt itself should be placed on the east side of the public road.

Further progress was reported at the first Board meeting of 1910, held on 18th January, at the Town Hall, Lampeter. Following lengthy negotiations with both the County Council and local landowners, an understanding was reached as to the most favourable site for the station at Aberayron. It was also agreed to purchase 3 roods, 12 perches of land required for this site from a certain David Evans, at a cost of £175. By April a detailed station plan for Aberayron had been settled with the GWR, and approved by the Directors.

Meanwhile further negotiations were taking place with the GWR regarding the junction with the Manchester & Milford line north of Lampeter. As these were proving difficult, the Board empowered F.D. Harford to find a settlement with J.C. Inglis, the Great Western Chairman, at a meeting at Paddington. This must have been successful, because in March it was noted that the GWR had agreed to deduct £150 from its charges in relation to the embankment. The company very promptly paid the balance of the sum required by the GWR for the junction. At the same time payment was made for other items, including ballast, and the Engineer was authorized to obtain up to 25,000 cu. yards of ballast in total. In April the Board was delighted to learn that the Treasury had approved a free grant of £10,000 under S.5 of the Light Railways Act, 1896. By now Captain Herbert Vaughan had resigned from the Board, and Mr Roger Lloyd and Major John Vaughan had been elected Directors.

The contractor and the Engineer clearly had a good working relationship, and construction continued steadily through 1910. On 19th April the Engineer reported that 7 miles 7 furlongs of track had been laid, and he also produced a plan showing amended arrangements for a halt and siding at Blaenplwyf. On 28th June he had further plans to show, these being of Aberayron, Ystrad, Ciliau, Talsarn and Silian. He advised that 'fair progress has been made, especially at the Aberayron end, and also that the permanent way is laid for 10 miles, bottom ballast for 6 and top ballast for 1 mile'. Most of the outstanding questions in relation to sidings and platforms had now been settled, and the first section of line from the junction to Ystrad was nearing completion. As the Directors naturally hoped to begin to recoup costs as soon as possible, Col Davies Evans suggested that a formal application be sent to the Board of Trade to inspect this section. The Board agreed, and the Engineer was asked to inform the Chairman

The terminus at Aberayron still under construction; notice the sidings have yet to be completed. A contractor's train stands at the platform. *Lens of Sutton*

The opening of the railway to Aberayron - Mrs Alban Gwynne cuts the silken cord across the platform, 12th May, 1911. *Ceredigion Museum, Aberystwyth*

when it was ready, so that the Directors might inspect and travel over it before any visit was made by Board of Trade officials.

This optimism soon met with disappointment. On 26th July the Chairman reported that the Board of Trade was willing to inspect the line to Ystrad, but the GWR was not willing to open until the line had been completed to Aberayron. The Great Western was probably concerned to ensure that the local directorate should not relax their efforts to complete their task, but the Directors were far from happy. They resolved that pending satisfactory arrangements with the GWR's Engineer they should carry out as little as possible of that company's additional requirements, although they were determined that the work to be done should be consistent with ultimately carrying them out. In truth the Great Western was not unhelpful, and was probably only seeking to safeguard its own position. In addition to providing track and ballast, the GWR also offered to supply station nameboards. This offer was accepted.

A month later, on 23rd August, the Engineer reported that the track had been laid to the bridge at Aberayron, and that the permanent way was complete as far as Ystrad. Of the remaining 6 miles, 4½ had received bottom ballast. Subject to the prompt provision of the remaining ballast, a representative of the contractor promised to finish the line in the shortest possible time.

The sense of urgency was now palpable. In late September the immediate erection of buildings at Aberayron and Ystrad was ordered, although the cost for both was not to exceed a modest £370. The contractor was asked to give priority to completing the platforms (rather than the shelters) at Ciliau, Talsarn, Blaenplwyf and Silian, and to complete the station and bridge work with the least possible delay. By now the Directors had every hope of persuading the Board of Trade to pass the line for public traffic within a few weeks. As in other aspects of the venture, aspiration ran ahead of reality. The contractor still had much to do. For example, the girders for the bridge at Aberayron had arrived, but still awaited installation; top ballasting had been completed over just 10 miles of track; the vital matter of signalling the line had not begun. The idea of a Board of Trade inspection late in the year soon faded.

In 1910 farmers and other residents near Ystrad took the trouble to petition the light railway company for siding accommodation for at least six wagons at Penwern. The Board felt that as the gradient of the line and the steepness of the approach road made Penwern unsuitable for sidings, the request should be dealt with by providing additional accommodation at Ystrad. The construction of a halt at Penwern was given more sympathetic consideration, and in October platform extensions at Penwern, Ciliau, Silian and, if possible Blaenplwyf, were mentioned. This was not enough to mollify the Penwern petitioners. On 6th December a deputation was received from the parish of Trefilan and Talsarn to discuss a siding at Penwern. The Chairman, J.C. Harford, explained the financial and practical implications, and made an offer 'that if after 12 months from opening the people of Talsarn do not find Ystrad convenient, and still wish to have a siding at Penwern, and the Board of Trade allow it, the Directors would do their utmost to find the capital, or would press the GWR, to make it'. This offer was later endorsed by the full Board, but somewhat surprisingly after so much discussion, it appears that the petitioners had to make do with the halt

An early view of Aberayron station, the sidings have still to reach their full extent, and the yard crane has yet to be erected.
Lens of Sutton

Loading timber at Aberayron in the early years of the railway. Timber traffic became a regular sight on the line, much of it going to the South Wales coalfield for pit props.
Ceredigion Museum, Aberystwyth

at Talsarn, and the siding space provided at Ystrad. It is believed that the siting of the halt at Talsarn was determined by the wishes of local landowners named Lewes.

The notion of petitioning the company for better facilities now became fashionable in the Aeron valley. On 20th December the Directors received a deputation from the parishes of Henfynyw and Llanarth, who had hopes of a halt at Neuaddlwyd, between Ciliau and Aberayron. It appears that the company accepted their case, at least in principle. Not to be outdone, other councillors representing the small parish of Llanbadarn Trefeglwys and Cilcenin put in a request for cattle loading facilities at Neuadd Ddu. Once again no mention was made of the cost of such an amenity, and the Directors, seemingly unaware of the thinking of the Board of Trade, suggested that it might be possible to load cattle and horses from the ordinary passenger platforms.

By January 1911, the Engineer was able to report that the contractor had practically completed the contract, with the exception of about five train loads of ballast. The station buildings were up, and the shelters for four halts had arrived and would be erected within a matter of days. The Engineer referred to subsidence in a cutting near Llanayron House which was spreading onto the line, and the contractor was asked to deal with it.

In the same week the Chairman advised the Board that under their working agreement with the GWR, there were several items outstanding. An engine shed was required at Aberayron, cattle pens and extra siding accommodation were wanted at both Aberayron and Ystrad, and a halt had to be built at Neuadd Lwyd. Whilst the Directors seem to have accepted the need for these items, they did not wish to meet GWR proposals to spend £1,500 on more ballast, and £1,100 on additional signalling. The Great Western, for its part, still did not share the local company's sense of urgency over opening the line, because it emerged that it had refused to lend two locomotives required by the Board of Trade inspector to test the new bridge at Aberayron. The company's solicitors were asked to sort the matter out, but in fairness to the GWR it must be said that the smaller company's extreme reluctance to spend a penny more than necessary must have been very irritating.

Fortunately this somewhat tense period was eased by fresh negotiations with the GWR. On 2nd February the Chairman was able to tell his fellow Directors that the GWR would take £500 in debentures to help the company complete the line, and that Paddington would now co-operate as regards the Board of Trade inspection. Indeed, an agreement with the GWR had been signed on 24th January, whereby that company had offered further financial assistance to enable the line to be completed to its satisfaction. The local company, in turn, had to arrange for the contractor's withdrawal. On 27th January Messrs Yockney and the GWR Engineer had been over the line together to reassess the works outstanding and the costs involved. As a result the Aberayron Directors were asked to give their personal indemnity against any claims that might yet arise from local landowners.

When the Board met on 24th March a good deal of progress had been made, although one or two matters relating to fencing and accommodation works were mentioned. The contractor had now withdrawn all his men, and the Board

An early photograph of a very busy scene at Aberayron. *Lens of Sutton*

A very heavy double-headed passenger train. The figures in the foreground are believed to have been members of the contractor's staff. Possibly this view was taken on the same day as the photograph above. *Lens of Sutton*

looked forward to the GWR taking over promptly. Although the Great Western required a debenture for £6,305 before undertaking the additional work they desired, this was agreed. Once again the Directors spoke optimistically of a Board of Trade inspection within a week. As ever, on the LA&NQ Light Railway aspirations ran ahead of realities!

The GWR came into possession of the line on 3rd April, when the district superintendent and other officials travelled over the new route in an inspection saloon. The next day, it has been noted, 'two heavy locomotives' arrived at Aberayron with 10 loaded ballast wagons. This generous provision of motive power may well have been intended not only to haul ballast but also to test bridges and clearances along the line. Even though the anticipated Board of Trade inspection did not take place immediately, it was found possible to open the railway to freight traffic on and from Monday, 10th April.

In fact the inspection was not long delayed. On 10th May the line was visited by Lt Col Druitt on behalf of the Board of Trade, and he advised that it could be opened for public passenger traffic. Arrangements for an official opening two days later were made hastily, and on a fine morning a number of notables assembled at Lampeter station. These included John Harford, the company Chairman, and other Directors, Mr S.W. Yockney, the Engineer, Sir John Llewelyn, a Director of the GWR, and Colonel Davies-Evans, the Lord Lieutenant of Cardiganshire. The party also included members of the Gwynne family, and most notably Mrs Alban Gwynne of Clifton, who had been invited to perform the opening ceremony at Aberayron.

Soon after 11.00 am the crowded Aberayron auto-train left Lampeter, and after stops at Silian and Blaenplwyf paused at Felin Fach. Here and at Ciliau Aeron so many people joined the train as to reduce it to standing room only. When the train reached Aberayron the platform was already packed, with spectators spilling over into carriages and wagons in the sidings, and onto the old bridge over the Aeron nearby. The station and its approach roads were decorated with flowers and flags and streamers, and the Lampeter Brass Band provided a hearty performance of 'Rule Britannia'. Soon after another special train arrived conveying more passengers from the stations along the line, amongst them the schoolchildren from Felin Fach and Ciliau Aeron.

The main task for Mrs Gwynne at the opening ceremony was to cut a silken cord stretched across the entrance to the Aberayron platform. Having received some silver scissors for the purpose, she duly cut the cord and declared the Lampeter and Aberayron Railway to be open. Mr Pennant James, Chairman of the Aberayron Urban District Council, then presented her with an inscribed silver flower vase as a memento of the event. A number of speeches followed, before the schoolchildren were invited to sing the Welsh National Anthem. They then returned to the special train to Felin Fach, whilst most of the public dispersed around Aberayron. The official party, accompanied by the Lampeter Brass Band, repaired to the Feathers Royal Hotel for lunch, and further speeches and toasts. In due course the dignitaries made their way back to the station to catch the 4.30 pm special train to Lampeter. At long last the railway was open, and the leading figures in the story had no doubt that Aberayron and the Aeron valley would soon see further progress and prosperity.

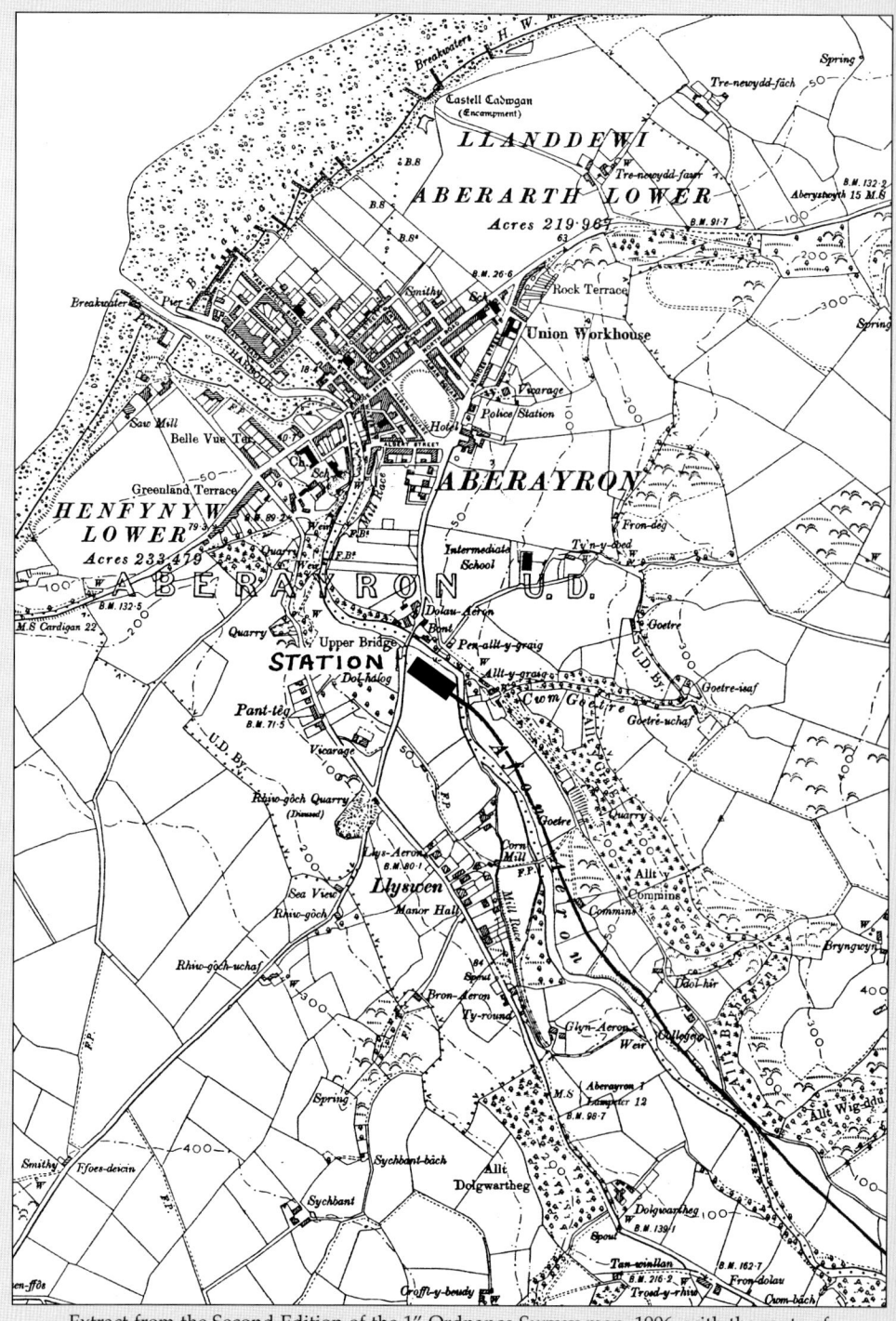

Extract from the Second Edition of the 1" Ordnance Survey map, 1906, with the route of the railway superimposed.

Private and not for Publication.

GREAT WESTERN RAILWAY.

R. 1387
F. 2040

PADDINGTON STATION,
May, 1911.

Opening of Lampeter and Aberayron Light Railway.

FRIDAY, MAY 12th, 1911.

On Friday, May 12th, this Line, which is a Branch from Lampeter, will be opened for traffic.

The Stations and Halts thereon with their respective distances from Lampeter are as under :—

Stations and Halts.	Distance from Lampeter Station.	
	M.	Ch.
Silian Halt	1	69
Blaenpiwyf Halt	4	5
Talsarn Halt	5	73
Ystrad Station (Cardiganshire) ...	7	24
Ciliau Halt	9	68
Aberayron	13	38

PASSENGER AND PARCELS TRAFFIC.

For particulars of Rail Motor Service see separate handbill. Through rates and fares will be supplied as required.

Parcels may be booked through to or from your Station and Silian Halt, Ystrad (Cardiganshire), Ciliau Halt, and Aberayron at the Clearing House scale and must be treated as "local" traffic.

Passengers only will be dealt with at Blaenplwyf Halt and Talsarn Halt.

Insert Silian Halt, Ystrad (Cardiganshire), Ciliau Halt and Aberayron in alphabetical order on your Local Distance Card.

SATURDAY TO MONDAY TICKETS.

Saturday to Monday Tickets will be issued from and to Silian, Ystrad (Cardiganshire) Ciliau and Aberayron, and these Stations should be inserted in the list in Clause 2 of Circular No. 1715 issued by the Superintendent of the Line, on April 15th, 1907.

GOODS TRAFFIC.

Accommodation is provided at Ystrad (Cardiganshire) for dealing with General Merchandise, Mineral, and Live Stock traffic. Similar accommodation is provided at Aberayron, and also for Furniture Vans, etc.

At Silian and Ciliau there is accommodation only for "Station to Station" traffic in full truck loads.

The invoicing and Goods clerical work for Silian will be done at Ystrad (Cardiganshire), and that for Ciliau at Aberayron.

Cranes are not at present provided at any of the Stations, but 30 cwt. cranes will shortly be provided at Ystrad and Aberayron. Lists of rates have been issued for each of the four Stations; if any others are required, application must be made to your District Goods Manager.

The Company will only for the present arrange for cartage at Aberayron, and rates must not be quoted for Silian, Ystrad and Ciliau as including this service.

Invoices for Silian, Ystrad (Cardiganshire), Ciliau and Aberayron must be treated as "Local" and abstracted accordingly.

A scene at Aberayron station soon after the opening of the line.   *Ceredigion Museum*

A view across the station yard at Aberayron giving a good view of the yard crane.
Lens of Sutton

Chapter Four

The Heyday of the Railway

The new line was undoubtedly a novelty in this rather remote rural area. In the first month of operation over 9,000 tickets were issued, and by the end of the year some 49,000 had been issued. Suitably encouraged, the Great Western started building the new halt at Neuaddlwyd as soon as work on the sidings at Aberayron had been completed. Never very sensitive towards either the Welsh language or Welsh spellings, the authorities at Paddington disregarded local objections and called the new platform 'Llanerch Ayron'. Although officially opened on 2nd October, 1911, on the evening of 7th September, 1911 a train from Lampeter stopped at the platform to allow passengers to alight. On this occasion a party from Llwyncelyn Congregational Church had travelled out from Aberayron to Lampeter, but were permitted to return to Llanerch Ayron, probably because it was slightly closer to Llwyncelyn village than the terminus. Access to stopping places was not always easy in the Aeron valley. In the spring of 1912 Cilcennin Parish Council tried unsuccessfully to persuade the company to create a footpath alongside the line south from Ciliau Aeron to the Pontnewydd road crossing.

The optimism for the future which accompanied the opening of the Aberayron line did not allow the company to neglect present business. One month after the Board of Trade inspection Messrs Edward Nuttall became entitled to receive 1,000 ordinary shares, and another 336 allotted under their contract. After a long consultation with S.W. Yockney, the contractor initially refused to accept the Engineer's final certificate of the sums owing to him. Later a compromise was accepted, and on 11th July, 1911, the Board noted that the full amount of the settlement with Messrs Nuttall was £500 cash, 2,836 shares (which included some 1,500 shares previously allotted in 1910) and £2,000 in debentures. If this represented a considerable cost to the company, the accounts received a modest boost by the sale of the contractor's shed at Silian, and their huts at Penwern and Blaenplwyf, all for £34 17s. 6d.

At this stage the company's finances needed all the help they could get. In truth the final phase of construction had been paid for with a loan from the Great Western, and at the time of opening the company could not even meet the interest payments. Once again the undertaking was saved by the Directors in general, and J.C. Harford in particular. It is believed that the Chairman provided £12,000 from his own pocket, and following his example the other Directors found another £8,000. As economy of operation was obviously essential for all concerned, the Great Western employed auto-trains for passenger services from the outset.

Negotiations with the Great Western were necessary for a variety of reasons. In September 1911 the Engineer was asked to find out the precise amount payable for maintaining the line, and to try to get the GWR to reduce the amount of extra ballast it deemed necessary for widening the trackbed. In March 1912 it was reported that the Great Western wanted the Brynog deviation

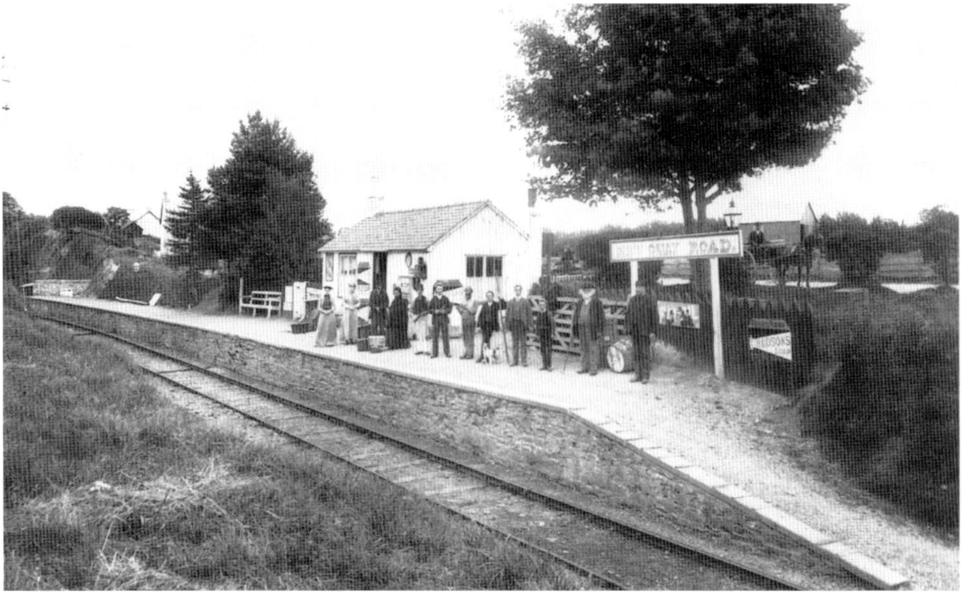

New Quay Road station on the Manchester & Milford Railway was 16 miles from New Quay. For some time before the opening of the LA&NQLR a horse omnibus service was operated from this station to New Quay. *National Library of Wales*

Gt. Western Ry.
Ystrad G.W. to
ABERAYRON
Third Class 1/0
FN See back
007

Gt. Western Ry.
Aberayron to
YSTRAD G.W.
Third Class 1/0
FN See back
007

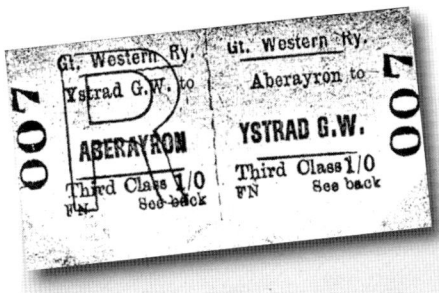

Left: A Great Western Railway return ticket from Aberayron to Ystrad issued on 12th May, 1911.

Below: A view of Ystrad station (renamed Felin Fach in 1913) with railway staff, a '517' class 0-4-2T and auto-trailer *c.* 1912. At this period there were four auto-trains in each direction each weekday. *Welsh Industrial & Maritime Museum*

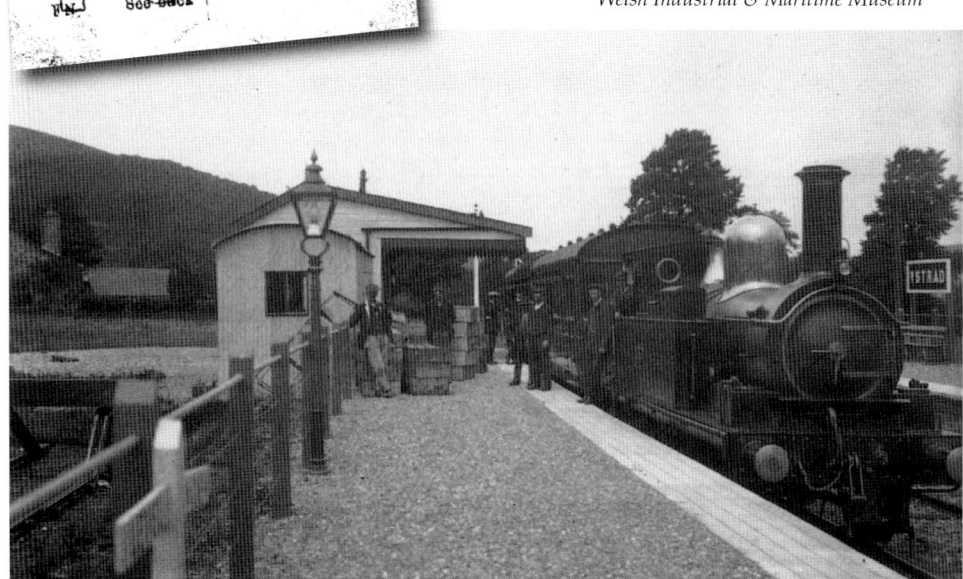

embankment, just north of Ystrad, to be raised - presumably to minimise any risk of flood damage. The Engineer repudiated any liability upon the company to do so. In the same month a national coal strike severely affected coal supplies throughout the country, and probably contributed to Aberayron rail services being considerably curtailed between 3rd March and 29th April, 1912. As a result the company requested that at such times the GWR's minimum rate for working trains of £250 per month be reduced. Although differences over the construction accounts seem to have been settled in 1913, negotiations over maintenance and working charges continued well into 1914. On the brighter side, the GWR agreed soon after the opening that they would issue free passes for the Directors and the company Secretary; J.E. Evans, the Secretary, cannot have made much use of this facility because he resigned at the end of 1911 and was replaced by J.D. Lloyd.

By 1914 old disputes and misunderstandings were gaining ground in Europe, and hostilities beckoned. As the stone of conflict was plunged into the pond of European peace, the ripples rolled out even into rural Cardiganshire. The most immediate consequence was the decision of the government to requisition railways from August 1914, to ensure that all railway operations took place with an awareness of national needs. The light railway company duly received an assurance and indemnity to the effect that the railway would be left in a financial position at the end of the war comparable to that experienced at the outset. The Chairman gave a full explanation of the arrangements to the shareholders at an annual general meeting held at the Town Hall, Lampeter, on 27th February, 1915. Soon after J.C. Harford was promoted to the rank of Major in his regiment, and departed to France on active service. Although he continued to be company Chairman, another Director, Major John Vaughan, resigned and was replaced by the familiar figure of F.D. Harford, newly returned from a diplomatic appointment in Venezuela. Early in 1916 Roger Lloyd also resigned from the Board, and Professor A.W. Scott of St David's College, Lampeter, was appointed instead.

Government controls, coupled with the Chairman's absence, evidently minimized company business for much of the war. Board meetings took place about twice a year, apparently timed to fit in with J.C. Harford's periods of leave. This was entirely appropriate, because there can be no doubt that the Chairman himself was keeping the company afloat financially. In January 1917, for example, he committed himself to act as guarantor on behalf of the company to its chief creditors. This was a vital contribution, because although traffic was maintained the company made a net loss in every year of its independent existence from 1911 to 1922. In 1912, following the temporary reduction in services and a notably wet summer, the net loss amounted to the very substantial sum of £962 13s. 7d. Whilst this was by far the worst year, in 1916 the net loss amounted to £453 4s. 0d. In short the Lampeter, Aberayron & New Quay Light Railway owed its very existence to the generosity and public spirit of J.C. Harford.

Three months later, at the annual general meeting of shareholders held on 23rd April, 1917, a resolution was passed which also pointed to the altered circumstances of wartime. Following requests from Aberayron, it was

A summer scene at Aberayron station before World War I. *Author's Collection*

The Lampeter-Aberayron branch train at Lampeter station in 1913. The locomotive is believed to be '517' class 0-4-2T No. 559, and in addition to coach No. 51 the train has been strengthened by the addition of two four-wheel coaches. This was a common practice at busy periods, and a couple of 4-wheel third class coaches were usually available at both Aberayron and Lampeter for this purpose. *British Rail*

GREAT WESTERN RAILWAY

Lampeter Pleasure Fair, Nov. 15th.

Tregaron Hiring Fairs, Nov. 18th and 25th.

Saturday, November 15th	Tuesdays, Nov. 18th & 25th
CHEAP TICKETS TO	CHEAP TICKETS TO
LAMPETER	**TREGARON**
BY ANY ORDINARY TRAIN.	BY ANY ORDINARY TRAIN.

FROM	Return Fares Third Class. s. d.	Returning from Lampeter same day at p.m.	FROM	Return Fares Third Class. s. d.	Returning from Tregaron same day at p.m.
Aberystwyth	3 9		Aberystwyth	2 6	
Llanrhystyd Road	3 6		Llanrhystyd Road	2 3	
Llanilar	3 0		Llanilar	1 9	4.5 or 8.0
Trawscoed	2 6		Trawscoed	1 3	
Strata Florida	2 0	3.40, 7.35	Strata Florida	8	
Tregaron	1 3				
Pont Llanio	1 0		Bryn Teify	2 9	
Llangybi	6		Maesycrugiau	2 6	
Derry Ormond	4		Llanybyther	2 0	
			Aberayron	3 0	
Aberayron	1 9		Ciliau Aeron	2 6	1.45 or 6.0
Ciliau Aeron	1 3		Felin Fach	2 0	
Felin Fach	1 0	3.50 or 7.40	Lampeter	1 3	
Talsarn Halt	9		Derry Ormond	1 0	
			Llangybi	10	
Llanybyther	9		Pont Llanio	5	
Maesycrugiau	1 3				
Bryn Teify	1 6				
Pencader	1 9				
Newcastle Emlyn	3 0				
Henllan	2 6	6.25			
Llandyssul	2 0				
Llanpumpsaint	2 3				
Conwil	2 9				
Bronwydd Arms	3 0				
Carmarthen	3 6				

CONDITIONS OF ISSUE OF EXCURSION TICKETS AND OTHER REDUCED FARE TICKETS.
Children under Three years of age, Free ; Three and under Fourteen, Half-price.
Excursion and other Tickets at fares less than the ordinary fares are issued subject to the Notices and Conditions shewn in the Company's current Time Table.

LUGGAGE ARRANGEMENTS.
CHEAP DAY TICKETS.—Passengers holding Cheap Day Tickets may carry with them 60lbs. of marketing goods at Owner's Risk, free of charge, all excess over that weight to be charged for. Passengers returning from Shopping Centres may take with them, free of charge, articles not exceeding in the aggregate 120lbs. (First Class) or 60lbs. (Third Class) which they have purchased for their own domestic use. Furniture, Linoleum, Musical Instruments, Cycles, Mail Carts, Typewriters, and other articles of a similar character are excepted from these arrangements.
DOGS ACCOMPANYING PASSENGERS are charged for at the single fare for the double journey, tickets available on day of issue only.

For any further information respecting the arrangements shewn in this Bill, application should be made at any of the Company's Stations or Offices ; to
Mr. H. WARWICK, District Traffic Manager, G.W.R., Oswestry ; to
Mr. J. LEA, Divisional Superintendent, G.W.R., Swansea ; or to
Mr. R. H. NICHOLLS, Superintendent of the Line, Paddington Station, W.

Paddington Station, October, 1930.   JAMES MILNE, General Manager.

trolleys used for track maintenance with what was then described as the 'Motor Economic System'. This involved the provision of motorized trolleys for use by track maintenance gangs, and the system was introduced from a point 4 chains from Aberayron Junction through to Aberayron on 8th August, 1932.

In February 1933, Cardiganshire was hit by the worst blizzard it had experienced in 50 years, and Aberayron was effectively cut off from the rest of Wales. Roads were soon blocked, and even the Aberayron branch was blocked, causing traffic to be suspended for three days. Eventually, on Saturday 25th February, a light engine managed to clear a way through from Lampeter, and it returned at about 6.30 pm with a passenger train. In the meantime a boat had been chartered to transport the mails between Aberayron and Aberystwyth.

In 1934 the hazards were human rather than meteorological. On 30th April that year a van driven by Gerwyn Jones of Llanybyther was struck by the 3.40 pm down train at a level crossing near the school at Felin Fach. The driver was shaken but mercifully unhurt. In September another local man, William Lewis of Blaenplwyf, was less fortunate. He was aged 73, and was deaf, and cannot have heard a down goods train approaching whilst he was stepping over the track at Cilerwisg cutting, west of Blaenplwyf. Mr Lewis was killed, and at the inquest the Coroner exonerated the train crew from any blame.

The Great Western Railway introduced its first camping coaches for holidaymakers in 1934, and by 1935 a camping coach had arrived at Aberayron. It is something of a mystery that the remote terminus at Aberayron should have been awarded a camping coach when (at this period) much more notable Welsh resorts like Tenby, Portmadoc, and Criccieth were not. Suffice to say that this facility did not last very long, because early in World War II all GWR camping coaches were withdrawn from public service, many finding use then for military personnel.

In the 1930s the timetable followed a regular pattern providing a basic service of four trains a day in each direction. In the summer of 1939 down trains departed from Lampeter at 8.15, 11.25 am, 3.40, and 7.05 pm, whilst up trains ran from Aberayron at 7.05, 10.05 am, 1.20, and 5.45 pm. In addition there was a service primarily intended for school children leaving Aberayron at 4.35 pm and running to Felin Fach, from where it returned at 5.00 pm. This service was operated on a 'Saturdays and school holidays excepted' basis.

Within a few months World War II had begun, and for the second time the railways were brought under government control. Although the branch was not subjected to the kind of frantic military activity seen on some parts of the system, a large military camp was established on the hills south of Aberayron. This brought numerous troop trains onto the line and additional military traffic. Unfortunately the full extent of these workings is not known because of wartime restrictions but it may have had some bearing on one or two track alterations at this period. In March 1943 the awkward siding by the crossing at Silian was closed and in November 1943 the passing loop at Felin Fach was lengthened by 22 yards.

During the war the passenger service was reduced to three return trips each weekday. This pattern was still in evidence at the end of the GWR era, in the autumn of 1947. In October of that year the timetable showed down trains from

GREAT WESTERN RAILWAY

Lampeter Agricultural Show

FRIDAY, AUGUST 22nd, 1930

CHEAP TICKETS to

LAMPETER

BY ANY ORDINARY TRAIN

FROM	Return Fares, Third Class.	To return same day at	FROM	Return Fares, Third Class.	To Return same day at
	s. d.	p.m.		s. d.	p.m.
Aberystwyth	3 9		Felin Fach	1 0	
Llanrhystyd Road	3 6		Talsarn Halt	9	} 3.50 or 7.40.
Llanilar	3 0		Blaenplwyf Halt	7	
Trawscoed	2 6				
Strata Florida	2 0	} 3.40, 7.30 or 8.55	Llanybyther	9	
Tregaron	1 3		Maesycrugiau	1 3	
Pont Llanio	1 0		Bryn Teify	1 6	
Llangybi	6		Pencader	1 9	
Derry Ormond	4		Llanpumpsaint	2 3	
			Conwil	2 9	} 6.25 p.m.
Aberayron	1 9		Bronwydd Arms	3 0	
Llanerch Ayron	1 6	} 3.50 or 7.40	Carmarthen	3 6	
Crossways Halt	1 6		Newcastle Emlyn	3 0	
Ciliau Aeron	1 3		Henllan	2 6	
			Llandyssul	2 0	

CONDITIONS OF ISSUE.

Children under Three years of age, Free; Three and under Fourteen, Half-price.
Excursion and other tickets at fares less than the ordinary fares are issued subject to the Notices and Conditions shown in the Company's current Time Tables.

LUGGAGE ARRANGEMENTS.

CHEAP DAY TICKETS.—Passengers holding Cheap Day Tickets may carry with them 60lbs. of marketing goods at Owner's Risk, free of charge, all excess over that weight to be charged for. Passengers returning from Shopping Centres may take with them, free of charge, at Owner's Risk, articles not exceeding in the aggregate 120lbs. (First Class) or 60lbs. (Third Class) which they have purchased for their own domestic use. Furniture, linoleum, musical instruments, cycles, mail carts, typewriters, and other articles of a similar character are excepted from these arrangements.

DOGS ACCOMPANYING PASSENGERS are charged for at the single fare for the double journey, tickets available on day of issue only.

For any further information respecting the arrangements shown in this Bill, application should be made at any of the Company's Stations or Offices; to
    Mr. H. WARWICK, District Traffic Manager, G.W.R., Oswestry; to
    Mr. J. LEA, Divisional Superintendent, G.W.R., Swansea; or to
    Mr. R. H. NICHOLLS, Superintendent of the Line, Paddington Station, W.

Paddington Station, August, 1930.   JAMES MILNE, General Manager.

Chapter Five

Under the Great Western

In retrospect it is clear that the LA&NQ Light Railway was built too late. Arguably, if one of the 19th century proposals for a railway had come to fruition Aberayron would have developed more quickly, and the surrounding area might have become more populous. In addition New Quay might well have received some rail connection. In the event, though, Aberayron obtained its railway at the very time that the internal combustion engine was becoming successful, and if the GWR had given the same thought to carrying goods by road as it did to the conveyance of passengers by motor bus, the case for the railway might have been undermined. Similarly, if Cardiganshire County Council and the various parish councils had decided to invest money in road improvements rather than the railway, there would have been little justification for anyone else to build it. However, judgements made with hindsight are easy; at the time no doubt all those involved were convinced that their decisions were sound.

In 1922 the light railway was completely absorbed into the Great Western, and the Aberayron branch - as it then became - actually managed to accommodate passengers for nearly 30 years more. It is known that in 1923 some 50,000 passengers used the line, but numbers soon began to drop in the face of bus competition. To compensate, some effort was made to attract passengers onto excursions to more distant destinations, although with only moderate success. It was also hoped to find ways of attracting more goods traffic onto the line, and in the spring of 1926, for example, negotiations were taking place for the delivery of 3,000 tons of granite to Ciliau Aeron for use on the principal roads of south Cardiganshire.

In 1924 the locomotive shed at Aberayron was severely damaged, it is believed by fire. Seeking an inexpensive solution to this problem, the GWR decided to use a second-hand shed! A short distance south of Wrexham Central station the Cambrian Railways had built a small shed for the Wrexham branch engine, but this had become redundant on the absorption of the Cambrian into the GWR in 1922. Accordingly this shed was dismantled and rebuilt in 1925 on the site of the old shed at Aberayron where it served its purpose well until May 1962.

The General Strike of May 1926 brought the railway to standstill by the suspension of train services. This caused considerable inconvenience, and, by way of example, horse dealers at the old Dalis Fair at Lampeter were affected badly. After some days a reduced service was restored, but it was not until the middle of June that trains began running to a full timetable once again.

In a further effort to encourage traffic the GWR decided to build a small halt at Crossways, between Llanerch Aeron and Ciliau Aeron. The work was put in hand, and the halt was duly opened on 8th April, 1929. The population of the Aeron Valley being very scattered, there was little scope for setting up any other new halts. Thought was given to making a few economies, and as early as 1926 Aberayron and Felin Fach ceased to have station masters, all the stopping places on the branch coming under the direction of the station master at Lampeter. Perhaps the most notable economy was the replacement of manually-propelled to the GWR (for a new access from the road to their warehouse at Felin Fach). By 1921, however, the main concern of the Board was the Railways Bill then before Parliament, which sought to create four major railway companies from over 120 assorted lesser lines. The Great Western was so much larger than any other undertaking in its area that it was to be allowed to retain its illustrious name, and absorb many much smaller companies - one of which was the Lampeter, Aberayron & New Quay Light Railway. By the time wartime controls were actually lifted from the company - on 1st September, 1921, - it was evident that its independence would be short-lived. Indeed, by the time of the annual staff dinner held at the Royal Feathers Hotel, Aberayron, on 25th March, 1922, it was realised that this would be the last such gathering under the light railway company's name.

On 27th June, 1922, an annual general meeting of shareholders, chaired by J.C. Harford, heard an explanation of the 1921 Railways' Act, and the preliminary scheme relating to the absorption of the light railway. It provided that GWR 2½ per cent debenture stock be issued in exchange for debentures in the light railway in the proportion of 1:3, and in addition the GWR would pay £8,840 in cash to the National Provincial Bank in discharge of the company's loan, and other liabilities. It was proposed that debentures held by the bank and by the GWR itself be cancelled, and also that the light railway's ordinary and preference shares be cancelled. As the company had never paid a dividend, these proposals provoked little debate, and were carried unanimously. A special shareholders' meeting duly approved the preliminary scheme, 'subject to such modifications as may be approved by the Directors and the Railways Amalgamation Tribunal.' In conclusion Mr J.M. Howell proposed a vote of thanks to Major Harford 'for the great services rendered by him in connection with the light railway, and to the County and other councils'. This was an entirely fitting end to the formalities, because a few days later, on 1st July, 1922, the company was taken over by the GWR.

A branch auto-train leaves Aberayron for Lampeter, *c.* 1914. *Author's Collection*

unanimously decided to ask the GWR to allow the times of goods and passenger trains to be changed: 'If the passenger train left Aberayron at 10.00 am it would connect with the 11.30 am train to Aberystwyth, and if the goods left Aberayron at 11.15 am it would suit the goods traffic better, giving farmers more time to get their stock loaded'. It was believed that this change was favoured by all parties, and would increase traffic. Furthermore, it was pointed out 'the discontinuance of the motor bus service from Aberayron to Aberystwyth makes the proposed alteration even more necessary as the 11.15 am passenger train does not connect with Aberystwyth'. The response of the GWR would appear to have been unsatisfactory, because in the later part of the war and for some time after it, the passenger service was actually reduced, giving rise to further financial negotiations between the light railway and the Great Western.

The coming of the railway had a marked effect upon coastal shipping at Aberayron, coal traffic transferring to rail especially quickly. Even so, the Aberayron Steam Packet Co. managed to remain in profit until 1915; thereafter its decline was swift. By the end of that year one of the company's two steamers, *The Norseman*, was up for sale. It changed hands in 1916, and was promptly wrecked on its first voyage for its new owners. Faced with steadily deteriorating trading conditions, the shipping company decided to go into voluntary liquidation in January 1917. The commercial use of Aberayron harbour was effectively suspended until 1920, to the considerable advantage of the railway. At the annual general meeting of the company, held in April 1918, the Directors were pleased to be able to report extra traffic on the line, partly 'owing to the closing of Aberayron Harbour', but also from an increased demand for timber, and the establishment of local cattle markets, as well as a flourishing mail service. In brief, although the railway did not succeed in making itself profitable, it did secure its place as the main supply route for Aberayron and the Aeron valley.

For some while after the war the Directors were anxious to win a cut in the GWR's charges for the period when passenger services were restricted. In addition they had at least one problem of a kind familiar in earlier days, namely an appeal from a local body (in this case the Vale of Aeron Co-operative Society)

A view of the railway staff at Aberayron in the early years of the line.   *Lens of Sutton*

LAMPETER AND ABERAYRON.

SINGLE LINE WORKED BY ELECTRIC TRAIN STAFF.

Sections.	Crossing Station.
Lampeter and Felin Fach .. .. .. Felin Fach and Aberayron	Felin Fach. Aberayron.

Down Trains.   Week Days.

Distance from Lampeter	STATIONS.	STATION No.	B Auto.		K Carmarthen Junction Goods.	B Auto.		B Auto. SO	B Auto.		B Auto.	
			arr.	dep.		arr.	dep.	arr. dep.	arr.	dep.	arr.	dep.
M. C.			A.M.	A.M.	A.M.	A.M.	A.M.	A.M.	P.M.	P.M	P.M.	P.M.
—	**Lampeter** ..	3741	7 57	8 15	7 40	8 55	10 57	11 25	—	1 40	3 40	6 17	7 0
1 24	Aberayron Junct.	3743		8 19	9 0		11 29		1 44		3 44	7 4	
1 69	Silian Halt ..	3824	—	8 22	O R	—	11 32	—	1 47	—	3 47	—	7 7
3 72	Stop Board		—	—	P	—	—	—	A				
4 5	Blaenplwyf Halt	3825	—	8 30	—	—	11 40	—	1 55	—	3 55	—	7 15
5 69	Stop Board ..		—	—	P	—	—	—					
5 73	Talsarn Halt	3826	—	8 37	S T	—	11 47	—	2 2	—	4 2	—	7 22
7 2	Stop Board ..												
7 24	**Felin Fach** ..	3826	8 42	8 43	9 30	10 30	11 52	11 53	2 7	2 8	4 9	—	7 28
9 68	Ciliau Aeron ..	3827	—	8 51	O R	—	12 1	—	2 16	—	4 17	—	7 36
10 60	Crossways Halt		—	8 55		—	12 5	—	2 20	—	4 21	—	7 41
11 7	Stop Board ..												
11 52	Ll'n'rch'yron Halt	3836	—	8 59	—	—	12 9	—	2 24	—	4 25	—	7 45
13 38	**Aberayron**	3828	9 5	10 5	11 0	11 20	12 15	—	2 30	—	4 31	5 25	7 51

A—Runs 5 minutes later on Saturdays.

Up Trains.   Week Days.

Distance from Aberayron	STATIONS.	B Auto.		B Auto.		B Auto. SO	B Auto SX	K Goods to Carmarthen Junction.	B Auto. SO		B Auto.	
		arr.	dep.	arr.	dep.	dep.	dep.	arr. dep.	arr.	dep.	arr.	dep.
M. C.		A.M	A.M.	A.M.	A.M.	P.M.	P.M.	A.M. A.M.	P.M.	P.M.	P.M.	P.M.
—	**Aberayron** ..	—	7	9 5	10 5	12 35	1 20	11 0	11 20	2 30	2 45	4 31	5 25
1 66	Llanerchayron Halt	—	7 11	—	10 11	12 41	1 26	—	—	—	2 51	—	5 31
2 57	Crossways Halt	—	7 15	—	10 15	12 45	1 30	—	—	—	2 55	—	5 35
3 50	Cilau Aeron ..	—	7 20	—	10 20	12 50	1 35	11 36	11 40	—	3 0	—	5 40
6 14	**Felin Fach**	—	7 28	10 27	10 28	12 59	1 43	11 50	12 35	3 8	5 47	5 48	
7 46	Talsarn Halt ..	—	7 35	—	10 35	1 6	1 50	S T	—	3 15	—	5 55	
9 33	Blaenplwyf Halt	—	7 43	—	10 43	1 14	1 58	—	—	—	3 23	6 3	
9 54	Stop Board ..							P					
11 43	Stop Board							P					
11 58	Silian Halt ..	—	7 51	—	10 51	1 22	2 6	—	—	—	3 31	—	6 11
12 14	Aberayron Junction	7 53		10 53		1 24	2 8		1 10	3 33		6 13	
13 38	**Lampeter**	7 57	8 15	10 57	11 25	1 28	2 12	1§15	1 55	3 37	3 40	6 17	7 0

§ On Saturdays leaves Felin Fach 12.15 p.m. and arrives Lampeter 12.55 p.m.

The crossings are provided with Cattle Guards and a white post is fixed alongside the Railway, at a distance of 300 yards on each side of the crossing. Trains and engines must not exceed a speed of 10 miles per hour, between each notice board and the crossing, and must be prepared to stop dead before fouling each crossing. The figure "10" appears on each post as an indication of this speed restriction.

Enginemen at Aberayron pose in front of a Collett 0-4-2T. *From left to right*: Mr E. Lewis of 'Trelawney' (fireman, then driver at Aberayron 1912-1944), Dai Griffiths of 'Gilfin' (fireman then driver at Aberayron 1918-1948), not known, then Victor H. Roach of Water Street (fireman 1930s). *Courtesy Aldred Roach*

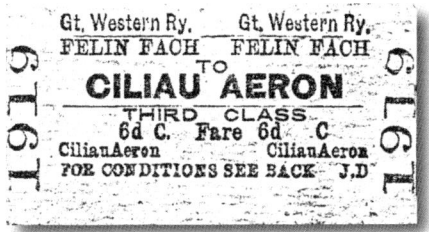

Lampeter at 8.25 am, 12.20, and 7.50 pm with an additional service at 4.35 pm on Saturdays. In the up direction trains left Aberayron at 7.15, 9.20 (Saturdays only), 10.55 am (Saturdays excepted), 3.00 (Saturdays only) and 5.35 pm. All trains were advertised as stopping at all halts although in practice trains would often only stop 'on request'. At no time were there ever any Sunday services, and under the GWR the branch was one of the more remote areas of responsibility of the company's Swansea District.

Before leaving the Great Western era it is appropriate to make mention of the railway tickets used on the line. So far as is known no tickets were ever printed in the name of the LA&NQLR. From the outset tickets were of standard Great Western design, Edmondson cards being issued at the stations whilst thick paper railmotor type tickets were issued by the guard to passengers boarding at the halts. According to Lewis Cozens, third class fares in 1911 were priced at 1d. per mile, but this rose to 1½d. per mile in 1923. Further increases were made in 1937 and 1940, these being followed after World War II by increases of 16 per cent in 1946 and 16½ per cent in 1947. The closure of the branch took place so soon after the creation of British Railways that no tickets appear to have been printed in its name.

Unfortunately the identities of the car and driver are uncertain, but it is thought that the driver could be the Aberayron station master. The private owner wagon is noteworthy because William Hubbard was not only a coal merchant but also the GWR's cartage agent at Aberayron. *R.W. Kidner Collection*

LAMPETER AND ABERAYRON — WEEKDAYS

Single Line worked by Electric Train Staff

Section	Crossing Station
Lampeter and Felin Fach ...	Felin Fach
Felin Fach and Aberayron ...	Aberayron

The level crossings are provided with Cattle Guards and a white post is fixed alongside the railway, at a distance of 300 yards on each side of the crossing. Trains and engines must not exceed a speed of 10 miles per hour, between each notice board and the crossing, and must be prepared to stop dead before fouling each crossing. The figure " 10 " appears on each post as an indication of this speed restriction.

Mile Post Mileage M	Mile Post Mileage C	Mileage from Lampeter M	Mileage from Lampeter C	DOWN	From previous place mentioned Ruling Gradient 1 in	K am	
—	—	—	—	**LAMPETER** ... ... dep	—	9 47	..
—	—	1	24	Aberayron Jn.	71 R	9 52	......
2	49½	3	73½	Stop Board	—	P	..
4	51	5	75	Stop Board	—	P	......
5	58	7	2	Stop Board	—	P	..
6	0	7	24	**FELIN FACH** .... arr	42 F	10 22	......
				... ... dep		10 42	..
7	6½	8	25	Green Grove Siding	500R 110F	R	......
8	44	9	68	Ciliau Aeron	100 R	R	..
9	64	11	8	Stop Board	—	P	......
12	14	13	38	**ABERAYRON** ... ... arr	74 F	11 22	..

Mileage from Aberayron M	Mileage from Aberayron C	UP	From previous place mentioned Ruling Gradient 1 in	K am
—	—	**ABERAYRON** ... ... dep	—	6N50
5	7½	Green Grove Siding	110R 500F	R
6	14	**FELIN FACH** ... ... arr	100 F	7 20
		.... dep		7 35
9	54	Stop Board	—	P
11	43	Stop Board	—	P
12	14	Aberayron Jn.	64 F	8 15
13	38	**LAMPETER** .... arr	71 F	8Z20

N—Shunt until 6.40 a.m.
Z—Shunt until 9.40 a.m.

LAMPETER AND ABERAYRON

The speed of any Train over the Lampeter and Aberayron Branch must not exceed 25 miles per hour, and must be further restricted to lower speed as shewn below:—

DOWN LINE

Aberayron Junction	Any Train through Junction	15
Silian Halt and Blaenplwyf Halt	Over Level Crossing at 0m. 47ch.	10
Silian Halt and Blaenplwyf Halt	" " " " 1m 11ch.	10
Silian Halt and Blaenplwyf Halt	" " " " 1m. 29ch.	10
Blaenplwyf Halt and Talsarn Halt	" " " " 2m. 63½ch.	10
Talsarn Halt and Felin Fach	" " " " 4m. 53½ch.	10
Talsarn Halt and Felin Fach	" " " " 5m. 47ch.	10
Felin Fach and Ciliau Aeron	" " " " 6m. 32½ch.	10
Felin Fach and Ciliau Aeron	" " " " 8m. 20½ch.	10
Ciliau Aeron and Crossways Halt	" " " " 8m. 46½ch.	10
Ciliau Aeron and Crossways Halt	" " " " 8m. 76ch.	10
Ciliau Aeron and Crossways Halt	" " " " 9m. 34½ch.	10
Llanerchayron Halt and Aberayron	" " " " 10m. 49½ch.	10

UP LINE

Aberayron and Llanerchayron Halt	Over Level Crossing at 10m. 49½ch.	10
Crossways Halt and Ciliau Aeron	" " " " 9m. 34½ch.	10
Crossways Halt and Ciliau Aeron	" " " " 8m. 76ch.	10
Crossways Halt and Ciliau Aeron	" " " " 8m. 46½ch.	10
Ciliau Aeron and Felin Fach	" " " " 8m. 20½ch.	10
Ciliau Aeron and Felin Fach	" " " " 6m. 32½ch.	10
Felin Fach and Talsarn Halt	" " " " 5m. 47ch.	10
Felin Fach and Talsarn Halt	" " " " 4m. 53½ch.	10
Talsarn Halt and Blaenplwyf Halt	" " " " 2m. 63½ch.	10
Blaenplwyf Halt and Silian Halt	" " " " 1m. 29ch.	10
Blaenplwyf Halt and Silian Halt	" " " " 1m. 11ch.	10
Blaenplwyf Halt and Silian Halt	" " " " 0m. 47ch.	10
Aberayron Junction	Any Train through Junction	15

Engine Loads for Branch Freight Trains

Section From	Section To	Working Loads: Maximum number of wagons to be conveyed except for Trains specially provided for in the Working Time Tables or by arrangement	Ungrouped 0-4-2T, 58XX Class of Traffic 1	2	3	Empties	For Group A Engines (except where otherwise stated) Class of Traffic 1	2	3	Empties		Group B Engines Class of Traffic 1	2	3	Empties	Group D Engines Class of Traffic 1	2	3	Empties
		ABERAYRON BRANCH																		
DOWN Lampeter	Aberayron	17	—	—	—	—	6	7	9	12	Auto.	—	—	—	—	—			
			—	—	—	—	9	11	14	18	0-6-0 T.M.	—	—	—	—	—			
			—	—	—	—	12	14	18	24	0-6-0 74XX.	—	—	—	—	—			
UP Aberayron	Lampeter	17	—	—	—	—	5	6	8	10	Auto.	—	—	—	—	—			
			—	—	—	—	8	10	12	16	0-6-0 T.M.	—	—	—	—	—			
			—	—	—	—	10	12	15	20	0-6-0 74XX.	—	—	—	—	—			

ABERAYRON TO LAMPETER (EXCLUSIVE). Route Colour—" Uncoloured "

Permitted Engines.—0–4–2T, 14XX, 58XX, 0–6–0T, 2008, 2012, 21XX, 74XX.
Local Restrictions.—Nil.

Extracts from the Freight Working Time Table, 17th June-15th September, 1957.

Chapter Six

Decline and Fall

The Railways Act, 1947, created a nationalized railway system with effect from 1st January, 1948, and the Aberayron branch became a tiny part of British Railways, initially controlled by the Railway Executive. At first there was some improvement in the passenger service, with four trains being provided each way. In the summer of 1950 down trains departed from Lampeter at 8.25 am, 12.20, 4.45, and 7.50 pm, whilst up trains left Aberayron at 7.15, 9.30 am, 3.00 and 5.45 pm. Unfortunately this service was not well supported, and according to Lewis Cozens the line carried only 7,000 passengers in the whole of 1950, implying an average of about six passengers per train. Not surprisingly, therefore, it was soon suggested that the service should be withdrawn. In October 1950, meetings were held at Aberayron, Lampeter and Aberystwyth at which BR representatives explained the case for closure to local authorities and other bodies. In every case these bodies resolved to oppose the closure, and in the Aeron valley the Lewes family in particular appeared to have good grounds for objection, because Talsarn halt had been provided for their benefit, and their consent was required before closure. In the event a severe national coal shortage in the early months of 1951 hastened the end of the passenger service, causing it to be suspended with effect from Monday, 12th February, the last trains having run on the evening of 10th February. The locomotive in charge was reported to be '14XX' class 0-4-2T No. 1472.

The main reason for the poor patronage was the allegedly inconvenient times of the trains, and in particular the lack of a late evening train from Lampeter to Aberayron. The official withdrawal of the service took place on 7th May, 1951, although the controversy surrounding the event continued. As late as 28th September the Transport Users' Consultative Committee for Wales expressed their disapproval, but to no avail. By then it seems that an understanding had been reached with the Lewes family in respect of Talsarn halt, and this was formalized by a deed of release dated 28th July, 1952. Meanwhile the replacement bus service offered by Crosville Motor Services was not generous, comprising only two return journeys per day between Lampeter and Aberayron.

Ironically, at the very moment of closure to passengers, an important new source of freight traffic was established on the line. By the beginning of 1951 work was under way on the construction of a milk processing factory at Green Grove, one mile north-west of Felin Fach. Built for the Milk Marketing Board, the new factory was provided with its own siding adjacent to the through line, and this was opened on 10th May, 1951. Milk traffic developed quickly, and it was deemed necessary to enlarge the factory. On 11th May, 1956, the then Home Secretary, Major Gwilym Lloyd George, formally opened extensions at Green Grove, allowing some 25,000 gallons of milk to be processed daily. After the ceremony, held almost exactly 45 years after the opening of the railway, the dignitaries (like their predecessors) adjourned to the Feathers Royal Hotel in Aberayron for lunch.

The Aberayron branch engine (*in the distance*) attaches milk tanks at Lampeter to the rear of the 1.25 pm train to Carmarthen hauled by ex-GWR 'Mogul' No. 6355 on the 7th July, 1958.

R.M. Casserley

Lampeter station, looking south. Aberystwyth-allocated ex-GWR Collett 0-6-0 No. 2260 is seen on a Carmarthen-Aberystwyth goods train on 11th April, 1959.

H.B. Priestley

DECLINE AND FALL 53

At this period Aberayron, Ciliau Aeron and Felin Fach remained open for freight, and the line was still remarkably busy. Cozens has noted that in the mid-1950s three weekday trains were operated in each direction. Up trains began with an early morning freight from Aberayron to Lampeter, which was followed by an up milk train at mid-day. Finally a late afternoon parcel and milk train was operated, conveying a brake third or parcels van (usually of BR Mark 1 design) from Aberayron. En route a stop would be made at Green Grove to collect two or three milk tanks destined for London, via Lampeter and the late evening service from Aberystwyth to Carmarthen.

The first down train to Aberayron at this time was a mid-morning freight, followed in mid-afternoon by a train conveying any traffic available. The last train of the day from Lampeter worked through to Aberayron, but consisted primarily of empty milk tanks. Had the milk factory opened before the demise of passenger traffic, this evening service might have become the basis for the evening passenger train Aberayron had been denied. On Sundays there was one up milk train in the afternoon, followed by a return working of empty milk tanks.

In view of the passenger closure it was something of a surprise when a camping coach re-appeared at Aberayron in 1952. Apparently the official means of access by rail travellers was by taxi from Lampeter or Aberystwyth, but it is said that unofficially those hiring the camping coach might well be able to get ride in the brake coach or parcels van which ran to Aberayron in connection with the evening milk train. Aberayron was not unique in having a camping coach, and no passenger trains. The passenger service between Alnwick and Coldstream in rural Northumberland was withdrawn as early as 1930, but in 1933 the London & North Eastern Railway began to offer camping coaches and other holiday accommodation in railway cottages at former stations. Some of these facilities were still available in the 1950s. In spite of its isolation, Aberayon must have been considered a successful site, because by 1958 a second camping coach had arrived. Unfortunately, though, British Railways' camping coach scheme went into retreat in the early 1960s, and Aberayron lost its coaches after the 1962 season.

By 1957 the freight service was in decline, and at Ciliau Aeron in particular traffic was negligible. The freight working timetable for 1957 showed just one train each way over the whole length of the line. This was booked to leave Aberayron at 6.50 am, and after a pause at Felin Fach between 7.20 and 7.35, arrived at Lampeter at 8.20 am. The return working was timed to leave Lampeter at 9.47 am and Felin Fach (after a 20 minute stop) at 10.42 am. The timetable anticipated that the train might stop if required at Green Grove and Ciliau Aeron before reaching Aberayron at 11.22 am.

Milk traffic, being passenger rated, the milk train service in 1957 was incorporated in the passenger working timetable. This showed a service operating every day, including Sundays. The locomotive, plus parcel van, would leave Aberayron at 11.35 am for Green Grove. There loaded milk tanks would be collected and taken on at 12.20 pm to Lampeter. The engine would shunt Lampeter yard before returning to Aberayron at 3.00 pm with another parcel van. Churns would be loaded into the parcel van, and a second trip

Camping coaches at Aberayron in July 1958. No. W9920W was converted in 1952 from GW No. 2458.
R.M. Casserley

Aberayron, facing Lampeter, with the locomotive shed in the distance. An ex-GWR 0-6-0PT stands near the water tower, 7th July, 1958. To the left can be seen the camping coaches.
R.M. Casserley

The signal box at Felin Fach station, 7th July, 1958.   *R.M. Casserley*

An award for the best maintained stretch of line is being presented to 'gang' leader, Harry Williams of 'Tegfan', Felin Fach, on behalf of his team, who are also pictured *c*.1955.
Cymdeithas Aberaeron Society

THE LAMPETER, ABERAYRON AND NEW QUAY LIGHT RAILWAY

F74 LAMPETER AND ABERAYRON

SINGLE LINE WORKED BY ELECTRIC TRAIN STAFF

Sections	Crossing Station
Lampeter and Felin Fach Felin Fach and Aberayron	Felin Fach

The level crossings are provided with Cattle Guards and a white post is fixed alongside the railway, at a distance of 300 yards on each side of the crossing. Trains and engines must not exceed a speed of 10 miles per hour, between each notice board and the crossing, and must be prepared to stop dead before fouling each crossing. The figure '10' appears on each post as an indication of this speed restriction.

WEEKDAYS / SUNDAYS

DOWN

								C		C		C		C	C	
						Ruling Gradient 1 in		E B V		Milk Tanks Empty		E B V		Milk Tanks Empty	Milk Tanks Empty	
Mile Post Mileage		Mileage from Lampeter						0B89		3F40		0B92		3F40	3F41	
M	C	M	C											Q	Q	Q
—	—	—	—	Lampeter .. .. ..dep		..	..	PM 3†0	..	PM 7 10	..	PM 2†45	..	PM 5 0	PM 5 30	
—	—	1	24	Aberayron Junction	71 R	..	..	3 5	..	7 15	..	2 50	..	5 5	..	Runs only when two trips are required for conveyance of milk
2	49½	3	73½	Stop Board ..	..	..	..	..	..	..	..	..	..	..	..	
4	51	5	75	Stop Board ..	..	..	..	..	..	..	..	..	..	..	..	
5	58	7	2	Stop Board ..	..	..	..	..	..	..	..	..	..	..	..	
6	0	7	24	FELIN FACH ....arr .. ..dep	42 F	..	..	3 30	..	7 40 7 55	..	3†15 3†16 3†21	..	5 30 5 45	6 0 6 15	
7	6¼	8	25	Green Grove Siding arr .. ..dep	500 R 110 F	..	..	..	..	..	..	..	..	..	..	
8	44	9	68	Ciliau Aeron ..	100 R	..	..	..	..	..	..	..	..	..	..	
9	64	11	8	Stop Board ..	..	..	..	..	..	..	..	..	..	..	..	
12	14	13	38	ABERAYRON ....arr	74 F	..	..	3†50	..	8 15	..	..	..	6 5	6 35	

WEEKDAYS / SUNDAYS

UP

								C		C		C		C	C	
						Ruling Gradient 1 in		Milk		Parcels and Milk		Milk		Milk	Milk	
Mileage from Aberayron								3F42		3F43		3F42		3F43	3F44	
M	C													Q	Q	Q
—	—	Aberayron .. .. ..dep			..	..	..	am 11†35	..	PM 5 25	..	PM 1† 0	..	PM 3† 0	PM ..	
3	50	Ciliau Aeron	100 F		..	..	..	..	..	..	..	..	..	..	..	Runs only when two trips are required for conveyance of milk
5	7¼	Green Grove Siding ..arr .. ..dep	63 R 110 R 500 F		..	..	..	11†55 12 20		5 42 5 55	D Shunt at Lampeter until 2.45 pm	1†20 1 45	..	3†20 3 35	4 5	
6	14	Felin Fach ....arr .. ..dep	100 F		..	..	..	12 25 12 30		6 0 6 6		1 50 1 55	..	3 50 3 55	4 20 4 25	
9	54	Stop Board ..	..		..	..	..	..		..		..	..	..	..	
11	43	Stop Board ..	..		..	..	..	..		..		..	..	..	..	
12	14	Aberayron Junction	64 F		..	..	..	12 55		6 30		2 20	..	4 20	4 50	
13	38	LAMPETER .. ..arr	71 F		..	..	..	1 D0		6 35		2 25	..	4 25	4 55	

Extract from the Working Time Table Winter 1961-62

DECLINE AND FALL

would leave Aberayron at 5.25 pm for Lampeter, picking up more loaded milk tanks at Green Grove for attachment to the 5.40 pm Aberystwyth-Carmarthen passenger train at Lampeter. Empty milk tanks off the 5.50 pm Carmarthen-Aberystwyth passenger train would leave Lampeter at 7.10 pm for Green Grove, and the locomotive and a parcel van would then return to Aberayron. On Sundays workings commenced with a train from Aberayron to Green Grove at 1.00 pm, going on at 1.45 pm to Lampeter. This returned to Green Grove, and if required would work a second trip to Lampeter at 4.15 pm before finally returning to Aberayron from Lampeter at 5.30 pm.

The weekday service of up to three trains a day continued until April 1962. In that month the branch locomotive ceased to be stabled at Aberayron, and the shed was closed, although it is believed that watering facilities were retained for a time. One guard's duty was transferred to Lampeter, to work the branch from the southern end with Carmarthen enginemen. Now a pattern of one freight train a day each way was established, the status of the branch having been reduced to that of a single line worked by one engine in steam. The locomotive came light from Carmarthen shed to pick up the train at Lampeter, the booked time of departure for Aberayron being 12.30 pm. At the terminus there was a pause of an hour to prepare the train for the return journey, and it was due to leave Aberayron at 2.55 pm.

By the autumn of 1964 Carmarthen shed had closed to steam, and so the locomotive now had to travel from Llanelly. The '74XX' locomotive rostered to work the branch was booked to leave Llanelly shed as early as 4.30 am. After shunting operations at Lampeter, the train was due to depart for Aberayron at the familiar time of 12.30 pm, reaching its destination at 1.55 pm. An hour later it left Aberayron, and apart from a brief pause at Lampeter at 4.35 pm, it ran straight through to Carmarthen and Llanelly - a full day for the locomotive, but one shared between Carmarthen and Aberystwyth enginemen.

A tiny piece of railway history was made on 16th May, 1964, when, for the first and last time, a three car diesel multiple unit visited Aberayron. The Swindon-built unit formed an enthusiasts' special organized by the Stephenson Locomotive Society; by the time another such special came onto the line the section north of Green Grove to Aberayron had been closed. The first visit of a main line diesel locomotive to Aberayron occurred in the summer of 1963, when a 1,700 hp 'Hymek' diesel-hydraulic was tried on the branch, and soon after a 1,750 hp diesel-electric of what later became known as class '37' put in an appearance. Initially these machines did not displace steam on a regular basis, but the closure first of Carmarthen shed, and then in 1965 of Llanelly shed, finally put an end to steam working on the lines north of Carmarthen.

The notorious Beeching Report of March 1963, proposed the closure of many Welsh routes, including the Manchester & Milford line. At this period there was less concern for the social implications of railway closures than for the narrower aim of reducing the considerable losses being incurred by the nationalized railways. Accordingly goods facilities were withdrawn from several M&M stations in December 1963, and very soon after the intended closure of the line to passenger traffic was announced. As might be expected, numerous objections were raised, but these were to no avail. The date for the

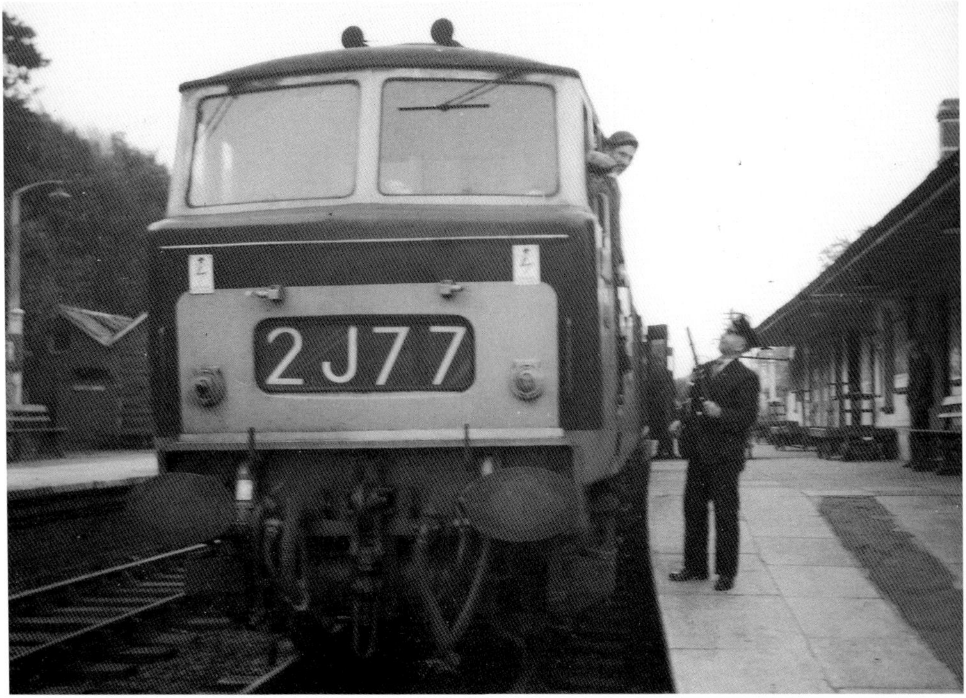

'Hymek' diesel No. D7034 at Lampeter station with the early train from Carmarthen to Aberystwyth on 13th September, 1963. These locomotives were used on freight services on the Aberayron branch. *Author*

0047
2nd - SPECIAL ARRANGEMENT
Stephenson Locomotive Society
(Midland Area)
WEST WALES RAIL TOUR
SATURDAY, 16th MAY, 1964
Llanelly (Sandy, L & MM), Tumble, Cross Hands, Tumble: Cwm Mawr (BP & GV), Burry Port (BP & GV), Pembrey, Carmarthen, Newcastle Emlyn, Pencader, Aberayron, Lampeter, Carmarthen, Llanelly, Swansea (High Street)
(W) (7817) For conditions see over
0047

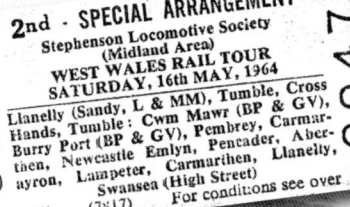

A 3-car Swindon Cross Country set at Aberayron with the Stephenson Locomotive Society railtour over the Aberayron branch on 16th May, 1964. *M.C. Bland*

Left: Ticket for the Stephenson Locomotive Society West Wales Rail Tour.

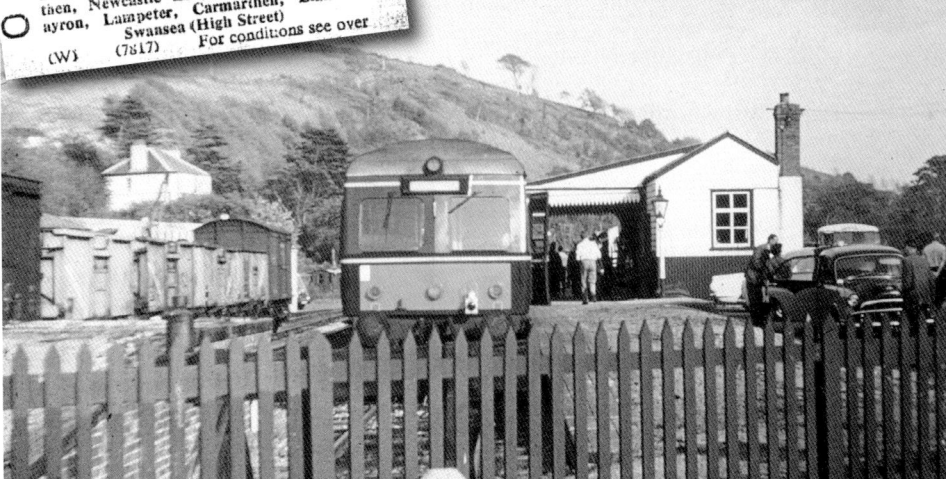

DECLINE AND FALL

withdrawal of the Carmarthen-Aberystwyth passenger service was set for 22nd February, 1965, when nature intervened unexpectedly. On 14th December, 1964, heavy rain caused the River Ystwyth to flood near Llanilar, washing out a section of track. Traffic north of Strata Florida promptly ceased, buses being used to complete the link with Aberystwyth. These arrangements ended with the official closure on the appointed day in February, leaving only the milk factory at Pont Llanio, together with Aberayron, Green Grove and Felin Fach, as the only sources of freight north of Lampeter.

In an environment so hostile to railways it was hardly surprising that the cuts in services on the M&M line were soon matched by cuts on the Aberayron branch. Indeed, Aberayron itself suffered the indignity of complete closure with effect from 5th April, 1965, when goods facilities were withdrawn at the terminus and also at Felin Fach. Even so, it is believed that the branch remained intact until early in 1966, when track lifting took place between a point about half a mile north of Green Grove and Aberayron. On 2nd January, 1966, the signal box at Lampeter closed, and the remaining portion of line to Green Grove was worked as a long siding, on the basis of 'one engine in steam'.

Lampeter station, as seen from a southbound passenger train from Aberystwyth to Carmarthen, with the 'Toad' brakevan and 0-6-0PT No. 7437 from the Aberayron branch freight at the down platform, 14th August, 1964. *Author*

60 THE LAMPETER, ABERAYRON AND NEW QUAY LIGHT RAILWAY

The introduction of main line diesels had an effect on the working timetable for trains to and from Green Grove. In June 1965, Landore depot, Swansea, was responsible for providing the 1,750 hp English Electric diesels for the two trains serving the branch daily. Turn 81 related to the 6.15 am from Carmarthen to Lampeter, operating trips to Green Grove and also Pont Llanio (near Tregaron, on the M&M line), before working back with the 1.00 pm departure from Lampeter to Carmarthen. Whilst this service was intended for general goods as well as milk tank wagons, Turn 77 was intended simply for milk traffic. In this case the train was due to leave Carmarthen for Lampeter at 11.20 am, arriving at 12.25 pm, and after trip working to the milk factories returned from Lampeter at 5.35 pm.

By 1968 the 1,750 hp English Electric diesels were regarded as standard motive power for trains to and from Lampeter, Green Grove and Pont Llanio. In the summer of that year the Working Timetable provided for two possible services to run on weekdays only. The service designated B71 was booked to leave Carmarthen Junction at 7.00 am and to reach Lampeter at 8.37 am. It then worked as required to Green Grove and/or Pont Llanio. It was due to leave Lampeter at 5.35 pm and be back in Carmarthen by 6.46 pm. On Saturdays it was anticipated that this train would head south from Lampeter much earlier, at 12.15 pm. Alternatively, if traffic only justified one train working north of Carmarthen, the locomotive on the Newcastle Emlyn service (designated B72) might be sent up from Pencader to Lampeter for milk traffic from Green Grove and Pont Llanio.

Once again these arrangements were not long lasting. Milk traffic from Pont Llanio ceased in the summer of 1970, and the line from Pont Llanio to Aberayron Junction closed officially on 1st October, 1970. With this reduction in business there was a need for only one train per day north of Carmarthen in the summer of 1971. This ran primarily to Newcastle Emlyn on Mondays, Wednesdays and Fridays, and to Lampeter on Tuesdays, Thursdays and Saturdays. This service was booked to leave Carmarthen Junction at 10.50 am, arriving at either Newcastle Emlyn at 12.40 pm or Lampeter at 12.10 pm. On the appropriate days the locomotive was required to shunt and work traffic to and from Felin Fach. The same Working Timetable also allowed for the possibility of a Sunday morning train to Felin Fach, leaving Carmarthen Junction at 9.00 am, operating only if the traffic made it necessary.

Within a couple of years this protracted story of decline reached its inevitable conclusion. The length of the lines from Carmarthen to Green Grove and Newcastle Emlyn amounted to over 45 route miles, being used by no more than one return working each day. Not surprisingly railway management sought to end such an uneconomic operation, and the withdrawal of the service was proposed for the end of 1972. Objections were lodged by the local authorities, and also the newly formed Teifi Valley Railway Preservation Society, and these succeeded in deferring the closure until September 1973. On 28th September the last freight train ran from Newcastle Emlyn, whilst the last milk train from Green Grove departed on 30th September, a final railway enthusiasts' excursion visiting both routes on the same day. By 1st October, 1973 the Aberayron branch was dead after a life of only 62 years.

Chapter Seven

Locomotives and Rolling Stock

The first locomotive is believed to have arrived almost as soon as track was laid at Aberayron Junction. Supplied by Messrs Edward Nuttall & Co. from their own stock at Trafford Park, Manchester, it was a typical contractors' 0-6-0 saddle tank, built by Hudswell, Clarke & Co., of Leeds. Unfortunately the precise identity of this engine has not been established, but a timber and corrugated iron shed was provided at Silian to accommodate it.

In 1911, as the line was approaching completion, at least two locomotives were borrowed from the GWR to test bridges and clearances along the line. One of these was an 0-4-2T of the '517' class No. 840; the other is thought to have been an 0-6-0ST of the '850' class. The actual opening of the railway brought another 0-6-0 tank locomotive to Aberayron. This was the outside-cylindered side tank No. 1356 *Will Scarlet*. Built by Fletcher, Jennings & Co. of Whitehaven (works no. 122) it was delivered to the Severn & Wye Joint Railway at Lydney, Gloucestershire, in December 1873. In its original condition it had wheels of 4 ft diameter, and cylinders measuring 16 in. x 24 in. It passed to the GWR in October 1895, and in the following year was extensively rebuilt at Swindon. A new dome and safety valve casing were set on a new boiler containing 214 tubes, and having a working pressure of 150 lb. The heating surface of the firebox was 86.9 sq. ft, and of the tubes 990.57 sq. ft, giving a total heating surface of 1077.53 sq. ft. Coupled wheels of 4 ft 1½ in. diameter were provided by the GWR, and the cylinders were slightly enlarged to 16½ in. x 24 in. In addition the water capacity was increased from 900 to 1,000 gallons, and a new half-cab was fitted. The tractive effort of the rebuilt engine was 17,820 lb., and its weight in working order was 39 tons 18 cwt.

By the time *Will Scarlet* reached Aberayron in 1911, it was not held in the highest esteem at Swindon. Indeed after little more than a year or so working on the new route the engine was sold to the Bute Works Supply Co., Cardiff, in November 1912. It was soon resold to the Alexandra (Newport & South Wales) Docks & Railway Co. and given the number 32 by that concern. Curiously enough, *Will Scarlet* returned to the GWR when it absorbed the Alexandra Docks line in 1922. By that time the engine had run an additional 141,663 miles and was deemed unworthy of further attention. Accordingly *Will Scarlet* was withdrawn in May 1923, without reverting to its old Great Western number 1356, and it was scrapped at Swindon on 26th January, 1924.

After the departure of *Will Scarlet* the branch was usually worked by an 0-4-2T of the '517' class, designed by Joseph Armstrong. At the time of World War I it is believed that Nos. 569 and 1444 were frequent performers on the line. By the beginning of 1921 two locomotives of the class were allocated to Aberayron, namely Nos. 219 and 847. Of these, No. 219 became better known as the regular branch engine. Built at Wolverhampton in 1876, No. 219 had 5 ft 0 in. coupled wheels and 3 ft 6 in. trailing wheels, and cylinders measuring 16 in. x 24 in. The water capacity of the side tanks was just 600 gallons. This

Ex-Severn & Wye Joint Railway 0-6-0T No. 1356 *Will Scarlet* at Aberayron.
The Late G.M. Perkins

An unidentified Great Western 0-6-0 saddle tank at Aberayron having made a remarkable attempt to extend the line! The incident is thought to have occurred in June 1912.
J. Percy Lloyd

LOCOMOTIVES AND ROLLING STOCK 63

locomotive also afforded the crew the comfort of a full cab, and it was fitted for auto-train operation, the usual auto-coach being No. 51. No. 219 was withdrawn in August 1934. Other engines of this class seen at Aberayron are believed to have included Nos. 205, 548 and 1157.

It is thought that several 0-6-0 tank locomotives of the '850' class visited the light railway, including Nos. 871, 1903, 1957 and 1959. Certainly No. 1959 was often seen in the period between the two World Wars. Built at Wolverhampton in 1888 as a saddle tank, it was rebuilt at Swindon in 1920 with pannier tanks holding up to 800 gallons. It had coupled wheels 4 ft 1 in. in diameter, and cylinders measuring 16 in. x 24 in. No. 1959 was taken out of service in November 1935.

In the 1930s two or three members of the brand new '48XX' class of 0-4-2T locomotives were seen on the Aberayron line. These were in effect an improved version of the '517' class, and had 16 in. x 24 in. cylinders and slightly larger coupled wheels of 5 ft 2 in. diameter. The side tanks accommodated 800 gallons, and the boiler pressure was 165 lb./sq. in. The tractive effort was 13,900 lb. Locomotives Nos. 4837, 4839, 4868 and 4872 were regularly used, but No. 4865 is also thought to have appeared. In 1946 the entire class was renumbered into the '14XX' series, and when the GWR gave way to British Railways at the beginning of 1948, the engine allocated to Aberayron was No. 1474. Several of these locomotives remained in use until the end of auto-train working on the Western Region of British Railways in October 1964. Indeed, No. 1472 was not withdrawn until 1964; no less than four examples of the class have been preserved.

It was soon realised that the '48XX' (or '14XX') class was not strong enough to handle goods traffic on the branch, and it is thought that the slightly more powerful '54XX' class of 0-6-0 pannier tank was tried on the line. If true, the experiment was short-lived, and before very long 0-6-0 pannier tanks in the '74XX' series were brought onto the route. This design, dating from 1936, handled the freight traffic effectively. Having a tractive effort of 18,010 lb., these engines had coupled wheels 4 ft 7 in. diameter, and 16½ in. x 24 in. cylinders. The boiler pressure was 180 lb./sq. in, and the water capacity some 1,100 gallons. At 46 tons 12 cwt., these were the heaviest steam locomotives to be used regularly on the Aberayron branch. Even so, they were a little less powerful than the '16XX' class of pannier tank, which had a tractive effort of 18,515 lb. The '16XX' class were designed by F.W. Hawksworth of the GWR, but not actually introduced until 1949, in the era of British Railways. Although the cylinders on this class had identical measurements to the '74XX' type, the six-coupled wheels were smaller at 4 ft 1½ in., and the boiler pressure lower at 165 lb./sq. in. The weight was 41 tons 12 cwt. As the '74XX' class remained in favour for the Aberayron line, the '16XX' variety was seen only occasionally after a short period in 1950/51 when No. 1624 was employed regularly. In the post-war period a number of '74XX' engines were used on the branch at different dates, including Nos. 7400, 7401, 7402, 7407, 7411, 7417, 7419, 7425, 7437, 7439, 7442 and 7444.

By 1963 the age of steam was fast drawing to a close in West Wales, and after the introduction that year of English Electric Type 3 diesels (later known as class

An unidentified Collett '14XX' class 0-4-2T is seen at Aberayron on a passenger train.
Lens of Sutton

Collett 0-4-2T No. 1419 is seen preparing to leave Aberayron with the 5.35 pm Aberayron to Lampeter train on 26th August, 1948.
F.K. Davies Collection

The '74XX' class pannier tanks were a familiar sight on the Aberayron line for over a quarter of a century. This is No. 7444 at Felin Fach, 7th July, 1958. *H.C. Casserley*

'37') most freight services were soon dieselized. It has been suggested to the writer that '74XX' locomotives managed to take care of Aberayron's goods service almost to the time Aberayron closed to all traffic in April 1965. This theory cannot be precisely correct, because the last of the '74XX' type was withdrawn in 1964. Even so, as late as August 1964, the present writer saw No. 7437 at Lampeter after working back from Felin Fach with a brakevan.

In the 1940s 0-6-0PT No. 7425 was a regular performer on the line. Unfortunately in November 1946 it suffered this spectacular mishap whilst working a Carmarthen to Aberayron goods train. The washout took place near Llanybyther on the Manchester and Milford line. The large man with a dark raincoat and cigarette (*left of centre*) is thought to be J. Vaughan Owen, the Machynlleth shedmaster. *G. Briwnant-Jones Collection*

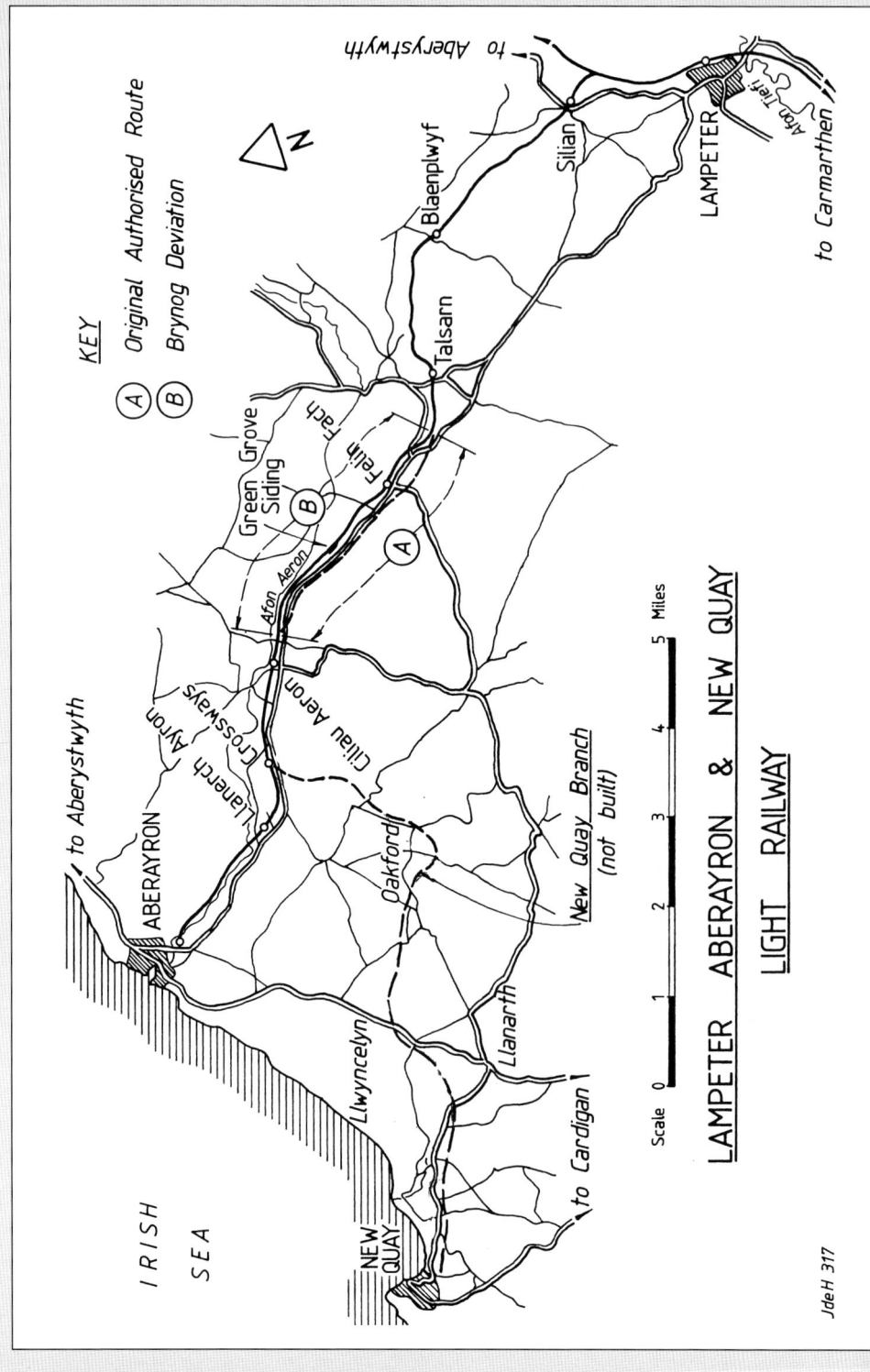

Chapter Eight

The Route Described

By Cardiganshire standards Lampeter possessed a large station prior to the completion of the LA&NQ Light Railway. Under the Manchester & Milford Railway it had been provided with up and down platforms, with a waiting shelter on the former and a long, low, brick building on the latter. These facilities were deemed quite adequate to handle the additional traffic offered by the light railway, and no significant improvements were made at the time the line opened. In the light of experience, however, it became apparent that the M&M's own signal box was sited inconveniently at the south end of the up platform. Accordingly this was replaced in 1916 by a standard Great Western box located at the north end, on the same side. The frame in this cabin had 23 levers, all but two of which were put to some use. Most controlled pointwork and signals in the immediate vicinity of the station and the extensive goods yard laid out just to the north, but eventually five were power worked to control Aberayron Junction and associated signals.

The Aberayron branch train would usually depart from the down platform, and was soon clear of both the goods yard and the town. After travelling just over a mile, mostly on embankment, Aberayron Junction was reached, the signal box being sited on the east side of the line. This small box lasted only until 21st August, 1929, before responsibility for the junction was transferred to the box at Lampeter. As the branch turned away to the north-west on a rising gradient of 1 in 71, the Aberystwyth line continued to the north-east, and within about a mile reached the small station of Derry Ormond (originally known as Betws). In a somewhat shorter distance the Aberayron line came to Silian Halt which, by being in the same parish as Derry Ormond, helped to provide the parish of Betws Bledrws with arguably the best rail service in the county.

The amenities at Silian were always very basic, comprising no more than the platform and a waiting shelter for passengers. At the north end the railway crossed the main road between Lampeter and Tregaron (now known as the A485), and until March 1943 there was beyond this level crossing a goods siding facing Lampeter. This facility may have been a reminder either of the construction period, when the contractor had his own siding and shed at Silian, or alternatively may have had some connection with John Harford, the prominent local landowner who contributed so much to the building of the railway. At all events, once past the siding the branch train began a steady climb through open country mostly following the Afon Denys. The final stretch to the isolated and equally basic halt at Blaenplwyf (2 miles 61 chains from Aberayron Junction) was on a gradient of 1 in 48.

Named after a nearby farm, Blaenplwyf, at 645 ft above sea level, was effectively the summit of the line, the railway crossing the watershed between streams running south towards the River Teifi, and streams running north towards the River Aeron and the sea. Indeed, once over a minor road the line soon passed through the short Cilerwisg cutting before emerging onto a ledge

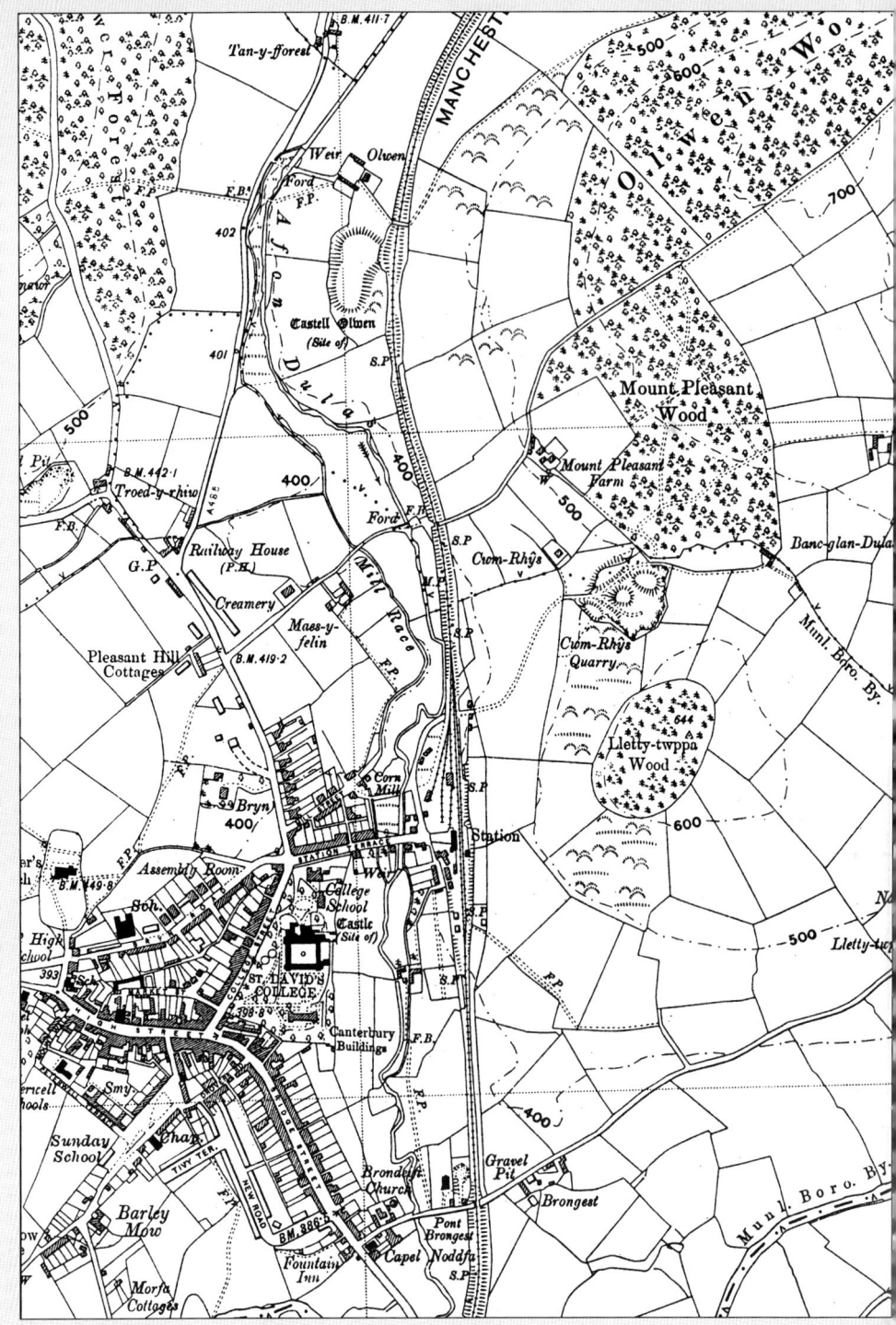

Lampeter station. Reproduced from the 6", 1938 Ordnance Survey Map

Two views of a busy scenes at Lampeter station. The view above is captioned 'Trucking, 1914, Dalis Fair'. While the lower view carries the caption 'Send off to a party of the 9th Welsh Regiment', presumably at a similar date.

Lens of Sutton

A view of the station building at Lampeter c.1910. *Lens of Sutton*

Another view of Lampeter station in BR days, this time looking northwards. *Lens of Sutton*

This view looks north at Aberayron Junction. The branch to Aberayron veers to the left with Aberayron Junction signal box on the right.
Welsh Industrial & Maritime Museum

Pannier tank No. 7407 is held at the branch home signal, prior to rejoining the main line at Aberayron Junction in September 1960. *J.I.C. Boyd*

Silian Halt, looking towards Aberayron, 7th July, 1958. *H.C. Casserley*

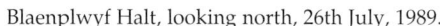

Blaenplwyf Halt, looking north, 26th July, 1989. *Author*

in the hillside above the narrow Nant Wisg valley. This was undoubtedly one of the most attractive portions of the line, and it included a wide overbridge at Cwmcafan. The track then followed several sinuous curves before crossing the substantial Hendrelas embankment to reach Talsarn Halt (4 miles 49 chains). This halt possessed the usual modest passenger shelter, and also, in the early days of the line, a small hut to give cover for the man in charge of the then gated level crossing just north of the halt. Indeed, the proximity of the halt to the roads from New Quay to Tregaron, and Aberystwyth to Llanybyther, as well as the road from Lampeter to Aberayron, gave rise to a number of unsuccessful appeals at the time of construction for the provision of a siding for agricultural traffic. In those days this spot was often referred to as Penwern; curiously it was named Talsarn after a tiny village about a mile to the north-east, whilst the nearer and larger settlement of Temple Bar to the south was overlooked.

The next stopping place also generated some debate about names. Originally called Ystrad, after the hamlet of Ystrad Aeron, it was soon re-named Felin Fach to distinguish it from other Great Western stations incorporating the word 'Ystrad'. Some 6 miles from Aberayron Junction, Felin Fach was always regarded as the principal intermediate station on the line, having a passing loop with two platforms, a fixed crane with a lifting capacity of 1½ tons, and the siding accommodation many farmers would have liked to see at Talsarn. These facilities justified the building of a small signal box with nine levers at the south end of Felin Fach station; the box retained its status until reduced to a ground frame in 1964. The station building on the down side was made of timber and corrugated iron to a most distinctive design, the passenger awning being an extension of the building's shallow roof line.

The construction of the Milk Marketing Board factory at Green Grove in 1951 altered the landscape north of Felin Fach. Just over 7 miles north of Aberayron Junction, Green Grove siding comprised both a siding and a goods loop. Small ground frames were provided at each end of the loop, and gates protected the access to the private siding. Although the ground frames were taken out of use in 1971, there can be no doubt that in the 1950s and 1960s the milk factory created considerable traffic for the railway and kept it alive.

Green Grove was located close to Brynog, the home of the influential Vaughan family, who had been heavily involved in the promotion of the light railway. The construction of the Brynog deviation in 1910 kept the line to the east of the Aberayron road north of Felin Fach, whereas the route originally authorized would have run to the west of the road, and partly in cutting. A short distance beyond this realigned section the railway reached Cilcennin level crossing and the goods loop siding preceding Ciliau Aeron (8 miles 44 chains). Apart from the siding, and one or two additional sheds on the platform, it cannot be said that the amenities at Ciliau Aeron were much better than those at the halts, but it was the only intermediate stopping place besides Felin Fach ever to be regarded as a station. Indeed, for much of the working life of the railway a man was appointed to look after Ciliau Aeron, including the level crossing just beyond the platform.

In the next mile there were three level crossings over minor roads before the railway came to Crossways Halt (9 miles 36 chains). As a late addition provided

The freight train for Aberayron passes milepost 4 with Talsarn Halt just visible by the trees to the right of the picture, 7th July, 1958.
R.M. Casserley

The bare platform at Talsarn, looking towards Lampeter. Note the simple cattle grids, widely used on the Aberayron line.
R.M. Casserley

Felin Fach (formerly Ystrad), with the the cattle dock in the foreground. View looking towards Aberayron, 28th February, 1959. Note the flat-bottomed rails still in place alongside the cattle dock and signal box. *J.I.C. Boyd*

A view from Felin Fach platform looking towards Lampeter. The signal box is to the right, 28th February, 1959. *Inset:* diagrammatic plan of Felin Fach. *J.I.C. Boyd*

Felin Fach looking looking along the platform towards Aberayron, 28th February, 1959.
J.I.C. Boyd

A pannier tank is signalled away from Felin Fach station with an Aberayron-bound goods train, 28th February, 1959.
J.I.C. Boyd

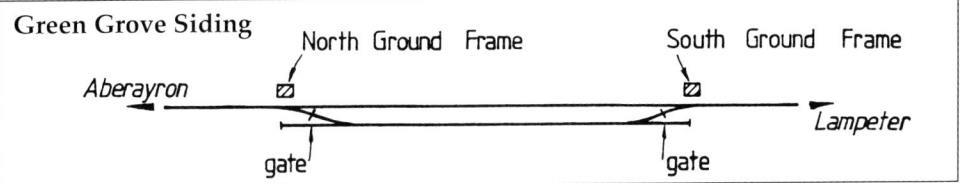

Two views of ex-GWR 0-6-0PT No. 7444 shunting the milk depot at Green Grove on 7th July, 1958. *(Both) H.C. Casserley*

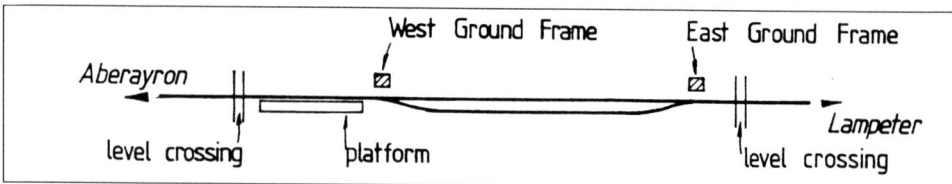

A view of Ciliau Aeron station looking towards Lampeter, 28th February, 1959. *Inset:* diagrammatic plan of Ciliau Aeron.
J.I.C. Boyd

Ex-GWR 0-6-0PT No. 7407 approaches the level crossing at Ciliau Aeron with the eastbound daily freight, August 1957.
Revd R.W.A. Jones

THE ROUTE DESCRIBED 79

The halt at Crossways. The pagoda-style waiting shed had been removed by the time this photograph was taken. *Nigel Bird Collection*

by the GWR in 1929, Crossways consisted simply of a timber-faced platform and a typical Great Western 'pagoda' waiting shed. It was located very close to the spot originally envisaged as the junction for the abortive branch to New Quay, but there is no evidence that any extra land was acquired with this possibility in mind. Just under a mile further north along the Aeron valley the line dropped at 1 in 40 to Llanerch Ayron Halt (10 miles 28 chains), which was described at its opening as having a platform 120 ft long, 12 ft wide and 3 ft high, a waiting shelter, lamps and a nameboard.

Leaving Llanerch Ayron the line crossed the Mydr, a tributary of the Aeron, by a girder bridge, before descending through increasingly wooded country alongside the Aeron towards Aberayron and the coast. On the last curve before reaching the terminus points marked the start of a lengthy run-round loop, and the locomotive shed appeared on the north-east side of the line, with a coal stage on an adjoining short spur. The two tracks forming the loop then crossed the river on a steel girder bridge, the track on the left running into the 130 yds-long platform whilst the track on the right threw off sidings known as No. 1, No. 2 and 'Coal'. Two sheds stood adjacent to the coal siding, the older one made of corrugated iron and the other, a grain store made of concrete, built as late as 1956. Beyond was a weighbridge dating from 1912, whilst a fixed crane similar to that at Felin Fach stood alongside No. 1 siding. A small signal box containing six levers was located between the river bridge and the passenger platform, which supported a station building very similar to that provided at

A view from the train showing the platform at Llanerch Ayron, looking towards Lampeter.
H.C. Casserley

Ex-GWR 0-6-0PT No. 7444 shunts at Aberayron on 7th July, 1958.
H.C. Casserley

THE ROUTE DESCRIBED

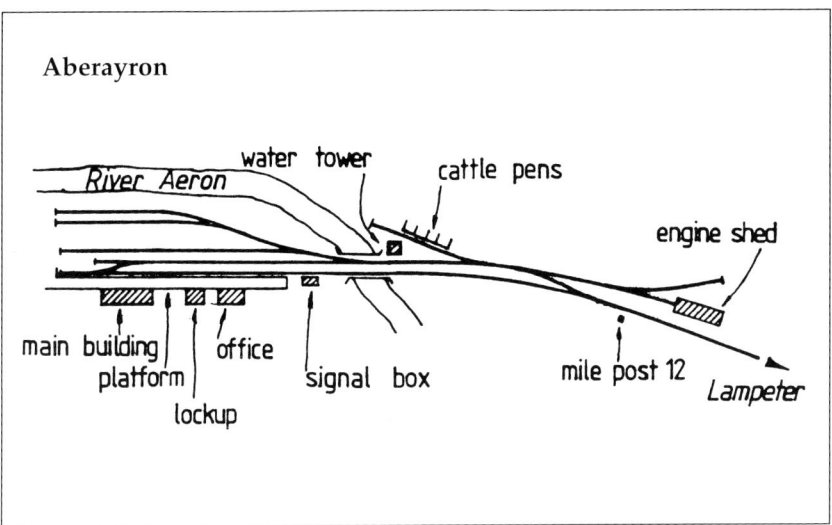

Felin Fach, together with a couple of sheds and the usual oil lamps. Although at the time of promotion some suggested that the line should run into the town of Aberayron, or even to the harbour, in the event rail passengers could hardly get a glimpse of the sea, and no train got closer to the coast than the GWR saddle tank which once ran through the buffers by about 30 feet. Needless to say, this unofficial extension of the branch was quickly rectified!

'74XX' class 0-6-0PT No. 7444 stands by the water tower at Aberayron on 18th June, 1963.
H.C. Casserley

A rear view of Aberayron shed, 7th July, 1958.   R.M. Casserley

Aberayron shed after closure, 18th June, 1963.   H.C. Casserley

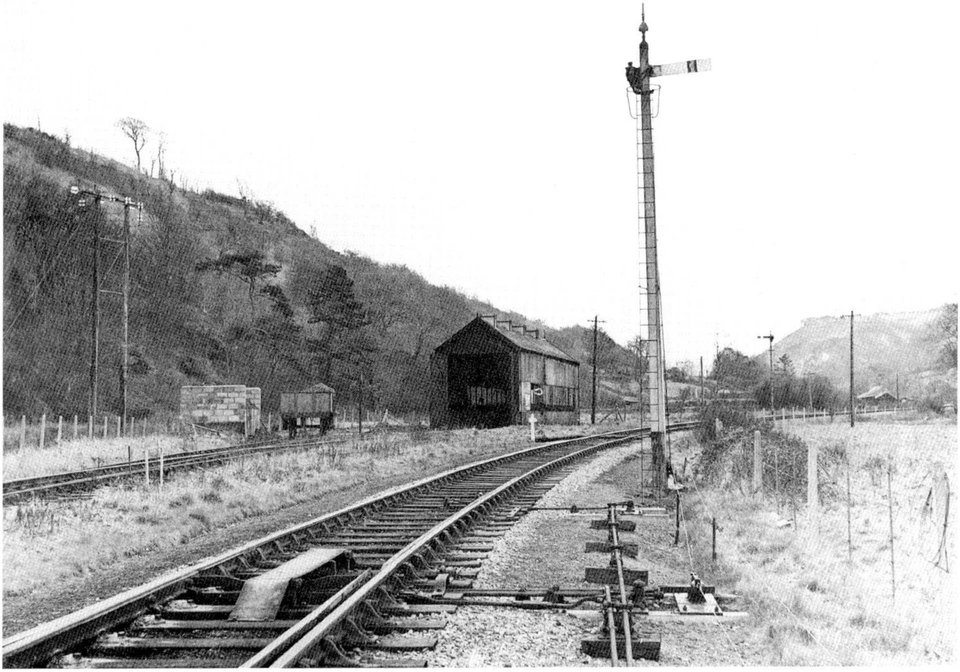

Two views of the station throat at Aberayron looking towards the engine shed and Lampeter, 28th February, 1959. *(Both) J.I.C. Boyd*

84 THE LAMPETER, ABERAYRON AND NEW QUAY LIGHT RAILWAY

Aberayron station and signal box, 7th July, 1958. *H.C. Casserley*

Aberayron signal box, 28th February, 1959. *J.I.C. Boyd*

THE ROUTE DESCRIBED

Pannier tank No. 7444 stands in the platform at Aberayron with its train on 7th July, 1958.
R.M. Casserley

The last days of the Aberayron line. Aberayron station seen from the buffer stops on 17th August, 1963.
Author

Ex-GWR 0-6-0PT No. 7407 shunts the goods yard at Aberayron station in September 1960.
J.I.C. Boyd

Agricultural and livestock traffic continued for many years after World War II. This horse was loaded at Aberayron in July 1958.
H.C. Casserley

Chapter Nine

Postscript

After the closure of the line, the track remained undisturbed for well over a year. In the spring of 1975 demolition began between Felin Fach and Lampeter, and proceeded southwards. Before long dismantling was also taking place on the Newcastle Emlyn branch, and throughout that summer the rails retreated towards Carmarthen. Eventually on 10th October, 1975, the track was lifted south of Abergwili Junction, near Carmarthen Goods, leaving only a mile of line *in situ* at Bronwydd Arms for the newly formed Gwili Railway.

Over most of the Aberayron route there were few changes for several years after the removal of track. In March 1981, for example, the station building at Felin Fach was largely intact, and the hand crane could still be seen in the goods yard. A short distance to the south track could still be seen in the road at the former level crossing, although this was lifted in the same month. Further south the old platform at Talsarn was undamaged but overgrown, and a broken railway sign was concealed in the boscage.

As the 1980s advanced more significant changes took place. The last plots of railway land were sold off, in most cases to farmers or adjoining landowners, and the sites of some of the stations were redeveloped. At Aberayron the station and goods yard was divided between two principal occupiers. The Welsh Water Board built a depot and offices on the land closest to the public road, for a time leaving part of the edge of the old platform visible in the depot yard. The railway bridge over the River Aeron became a road bridge giving access to a depot owned by Jewsons, builders merchants. By then the small signal box had been sold, and moved to a private garden at Fishguard. In 1985 a section of the trackbed south towards Llanerch Ayron became a popular public footpath. The alignment for a short distance beyond, almost to Crossways, became a permissive path.

At Ciliau Aeron the station site was redeveloped as a small housing estate named Maes Aeron. In 1987 the station building at Felin Fach was moved by the Gwili Railway Preservation Society to their line at Llwyfan Cerrig, where it was rebuilt to serve the same purpose for which it had been designed. Meanwhile it was replaced at Felin Fach by new buildings for the Cardiganshire Farmers' Co-operative. Soon after the trackbed south to the level crossing site was redeveloped as a small cul-de-sac of bungalows, appropriately named Maes y Tren.

The 1980s also witnessed changes at Green Grove. For some years the milk factory was operated by Dairycrest, a trading arm of the Milk Marketing Board. In March 1988, amid some local anxiety, the factory - then described as a creamery - was closed, and the site put up for sale. Fortunately the purchasers had every intention of keeping Green Grove in production, although for a somewhat different purpose. The buyers were Champlain Protex Ltd, a company specializing in hydrolysed vegetable protein products, including flavourings, intended to enhance a wide range of convenience foods. Faced

The last of the Aberayron branch. Following road resurfacing, discarded track from a level crossing near Felin Fach awaits disposal, March 1981. *Author*

The scene of desolation and decay at Felin Fach station, March 1981. *Author*

with a need to relocate their business from a site near the M25 motorway on the edge of London, Champlain Protex Ltd refurbished the Green Grove factory and re-opened it in their name in April 1989. In July 1994, the Universal Foods Company of Milwaukee, USA, acquired Champlain Protex, incorporating the business into their Speciality Bio Products division. In 2010 food flavourings were still being produced at Felin Fach, but the company now trades under the name of Sensient. The northern end of the old milk factory site now constitutes the small Duffryn Aeron Valley enterprise park.

If developments at Green Grove offer some hope of future employment and prosperity in the Aeron valley, the same cannot be said with much confidence about the rest of the route of the old railway. Much of the line has simply reverted to the agricultural use from which it was taken, although a few sections have become farm tracks to improve access to fields, for example at Crossways, Talsarn and just north of Blaenplwyf. Decayed and heavily overgrown platforms may still be seen at Llanerch Ayron, Talsarn, Blaenplwyf and Silian, but the largest station of all- Lampeter - has been demolished. Part of the goods yard was redeveloped as a cattle market, but the only railway feature still in evidence is the former goods shed. In 1984 this was refurbished and given a modern extension, and now provides offices for a local housing trust, Tai Ceredigion.

A curiosity of the late 1990s was the occasional appearance of Aberaeron (not Aberayron) on railway tickets. The Trawscambria long distance bus service from Cardiff to Holyhead was routed via Aberaeron and Aberystwyth, and became an advertised railway connectional facility. Accordingly it became possible to book a rail ticket in, say, Newport, and then transfer to the bus in Cardiff for the onward journey to Aberaeron. Given that the GWR had operated buses to Aberayron before trains, there was some irony in the full destination on the modern tickets being rendered as 'Aberaeron bus'.

Commemorative plaques marking the opening of the Aberaeron Town Council amenity scheme in 1985. This included the provision of a footpath on a section of the old railway south from Aberayron, 26th July, 1989.   *Author*

Light railway bridge in use as a road at Aberayron, 26th July, 1989. *Author*

Talsarn Halt (*right*) looking south on 26th July, 1989. *Author*

The site of the former GWR bus garage at New Quay. The land now occupied by three private garages was formerly taken by the corrugated iron structure used by the GWR.
Author

Since the creation of the Welsh Assembly in the late 1990s it has been suggested on several occasions that the railway from Camarthen to Lampeter and on to Aberystwyth should be rebuilt to improve transport links between South and Mid-Wales. Although desirable, it is clear that the cost of such an exercise would be immense. Given the severe financial constraints on government following the banking crisis of 2008, such expenditure is not likely to be contemplated. It is even more certain that the LA&NQLR has gone for good. In its day, though, it gave good service to the farmers and traders of Cardiganshire, and it deserves its modest but honourable place in Welsh railway history.

The former Aberayron signal box has been rebuilt in a private garden near Fishguard.
Bill Fowler

This view is said to be of lead miners at work in the Neuadd Quarry, New Quay, in the 1860s.
National Library of Wales

A view of the site of the lead mines in 1994. *Author*

Appendix One

The New Quay Harbour Tramway

At the beginning of the 19th century the only pier or breakwater at New Quay was located close to the modern lifeboat station, on the site of the present-day concrete jetty. This old pier was of simple construction, comprising heavy stakes set deep in the sand, and secured by large boulders. The need for a new pier was obvious, and even in the 1790s it was suggested that New Quay might be developed as a packet port for Ireland. In 1815 Walter Davies in his book *General View of the Economy of South Wales* emphasized the potential of New Quay as a harbour of refuge, and expressed the somewhat optimistic idea that £30,000 might provide a harbour of refuge big enough to give security to 200 vessels. In 1820 Alban Gwynne took the practical step of asking the engineer John Rennie to carry out a survey, and produce appropriate plans. Rennie was already well-known, his work including the designs for London Bridge, and also the Southwark and Chelsea bridges. Given this background Rennie's ideas were arguably too grand; they were most certainly too costly. After the death of Alban Gwynne it seems his hopes were kept alive for some time by J.J. Gwynne; a Colonel Jones of Havod also had plans for an improved harbour, but his proposals met with some local opposition.

On the evidence of a promotional booklet published in the year 1834, the Directors had high hopes of developing New Quay as a port for Irish traffic. It stated that the passage to Dublin would be some hours shorter than from Holyhead, and that the Government would probably adopt New Quay as the place of embarkation of the Irish Mails. A survey had been carried out by John Haslam of the Board of Ordnance for a harbour with 8 ft of water at low tide to take boats of up to 300 tons, the 'jutty' to be 60 ft from the pier face. It was noted that in July 1834 a steam boat plying between Aberystwyth and Pwllheli called at New Quay once a week. At this date the company capital was said to be £5,000, the estimated cost of the development being £4,300. It was envisaged that the works would require 25,336 perches of rubble slate and 5,846 perches of masonry.

By 1835 this plan was out of favour, and it appears that the designs of Daniel Beynon were preferred, although more expensive in estimate at £4,722. At all events, an Act of Parliament was obtained approving the construction of a large stone pier. The authorized capital amounted now to £7,000 in 700 £10 shares, and it was stipulated that the right to collect tolls should not be granted to anyone for a sum less than £160 per annum. The first formal meeting of the New Quay Harbour Co. took place on 30th June, 1835, when Captain James R. Lewes Lloyd was appointed Chairman. There were 13 other Directors, most of whom were gentlemen landowners. Soon after R.W. Jones of Loughor was appointed company Engineer for two years from 29th September, 1835, at a salary of £500. He must have been regarded as well qualified for the task, because he was almost certainly one and the same man as the R.W. Jones who supervised the construction of the harbour at Saundersfoot, Pembrokeshire, between 1830 and 1835.

The New Quay Harbour Co. acquired land for the pier from William Evans of Penywig Farm, and for a stone quarry from Evan Evans of Neuadd. From the outset it was intended that a tramway should be made to connect the two sites, and convey stone to the new harbour. Building work began promptly, and a certain Solomon Williams was employed by the company to open up the quarry on the nearby headland. Unfortunately in May 1836, Williams was killed in a fall whilst tipping spoil over the cliffs, but by then the tramway was in regular use. The line is believed to have been completed on 8th March, 1836. At its greatest extent it did not exceed half a mile in length, and for practical operational purposes it was little more than 600 yards long. It is believed to have been horse-worked.

The short section of 4 ft 2 in. gauge bar rail track set in chairs from the former New Quay Harbour Tramway, on view near the Tourist Information office at New Quay on 16th August, 1994.
Author

New Quay harbour and pier. The course of the New Quay Harbour Tramway has been superimposed (– – –).
Reproduced from the 6", 1887 OS Map

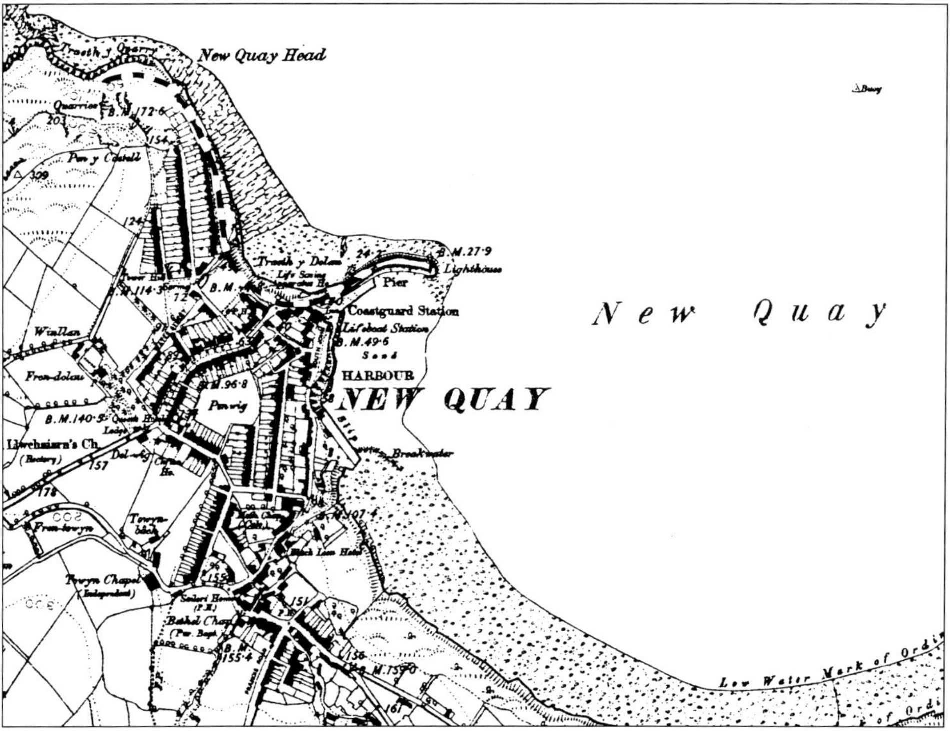

APPENDIX

By 1837 it had become apparent that for the harbour to be effective the new pier would have to be further extended. As the original capital had been expended, the company took out loans to allow them to finish the job. In addition they decided to collect tolls and dues at the harbour with effect from 1st October, 1837, and James Davies was appointed collector. It seems likely that the construction and consolidation of the pier and associated warehouses took longer than anticipated, and that initially the tolls and dues did not produce as much income as expected. By May 1838, just £129 18s. 7½d. had been received, and so it was decided to extend some of the tolls. As James Davies put his mind to this task it seems he also gained responsibility for supervising the final stages of the harbour works. It appears that the job was done by 1840.

Virtually nothing is known about operating practice on the harbour tramway, but whilst the construction of the harbour was proceeding in the late 1830s it was decided to develop houses along the route. This became known as Rock Street, and although no positive evidence is to hand, it seems reasonable to suppose that the tramway was also used to convey stone for the Rock Street properties. Indeed the very existence of the tramway was surely a major factor in favour of carrying out the work. Unfortunately it is not clear what happened to the tramway after the completion of both the harbour and Rock Street, but it would seem that by the mid-1840s it had fallen into disuse.

The earliest tithe map for the area that has been seen is dated 1848. As this does not depict the tramway it may be supposed that it was out of use. The quarry site (sometimes called the Neuadd quarry) was described as 'pasture', owned and occupied by David Evans. As he owned the entire headland, it is easy to imagine that he prospered both from the use of the quarry and from the development of Rock Street. However, some years later the tramway was mentioned again, because, following a massive storm in October 1859, it was suggested that the tramway should be restored to assist in carrying out repairs to the harbour. It appears that R.W. Jones, and his clerk of works, William Hopkin, were consulted about the repairs and estimated that they might cost up to £2,000. It is not known if the tramway was brought back into use for this purpose in 1860, but if so its period of service would appear to have been quite brief. After the line had been dismantled a short portion of track must have been buried in the quarry or somewhere along the route, because in about 1970 a section of track was preserved by the Tourist Information Office near the Harbour. This restored track comprises two lengths of bar rail set in cast-iron chairs on stone blocks; the gauge is approximately 4 feet 2 inches.

This is not quite the end of the story. It is believed that in the 1740s there were attempts to mine lead at New Quay, with uncertain results. In 1844 Evan Evans of Neuadd made reference to a lead ore mine 'recently discovered' - no doubt by the quarrying of rock for the harbour. However, no more is known of this working before 29th October, 1864, when the *Mining Journal* carried the following report:

> Mining in Cardiganshire - We have received from Mr John Rees of New Quay, a box of specimens of ore, obtained from the land of Mr David Evans, of Vrondoley [now known as Frondolau], and consisting of stones of lead in a matrix of quartz and mundic, embedded in sandstone, the minute crystals of mundic giving the stone a very pretty appearance. Mr Rees states that the rocks are very convenient for shipping, and deliver rubbish to the sea, the distance from the harbour being only about 400 yards. He believes plenty of lead ore could be got when the mines are in working order, and that the sett could be obtained upon easy terms.

It is said that there were mine workings at Frondolau, set back some distance from the sea, but a surviving photograph dating from the 1860s shows lead miners at work in the Neuadd quarry. In 1870 there was a published reference to a limited company called 'Wheal Neptune' formed to work lead at New Quay, and it is understood that this related to the same venture. However, no more is known of the scheme, and it is generally thought to have been unsuccessful. Today the quarry and some associated spoil heaps can still be found at the far end of Rock Street; the lowest level of the quarry is now occupied by the buildings of Quay Frozen Foods Ltd. Apart from the small section of preserved track, there is now nothing to show that the New Quay Harbour tramway ever existed.

Appendix Two

Extracts from the Lampeter Aberayron and New Quay Light Railway Order 1906

4. John Charles Harford and Wilmot Ingles-Jones and John Edward Rogers and Herbert Vaughan and Herbert Davies-Evans and William Griffiths and Evan James Davies and Evan Lewis and Morgan Evans and Jenkin Davies and Jenkyn Jenkyns and all other persons and corporations who have already subscribed to or shall hereafter become proprietors in the undertaking and their executors administrators successors and assigns respectively are hereby united into a Company for the purpose of making and maintaining the railway and for other the purposes of this Order and for those purposes are hereby incorporated by the name of the 'Lampeter Aberayron and New Quay Light Railway Company' and by that name shall be a body corporate with a perpetual succession and a common seal and with power to purchase take hold and dispose of lands and other property for the purposes of this Order.

Railways Authorised

11. Subject to the provisions of this Order the Company may make and maintain in the lines and according to the levels shown on the Plan and Section the make Railways hereinafter described with all proper and sufficient rails plates sidings railway junctions turntables bridges culverts drains viaducts stations approaches roads yards buildings and other works and conveniences connected therewith.

The said Railways are:—
A Railway (No. 1) [being Railway (No. 1) of the application of 1903] 13 miles 3 furlongs or thereabouts in length commencing in the borough and parish of Lampeter on the southern side of a piece of land No. 227 on the 25-inch Ordnance Map of the said parish at or near a point adjoining the public road leading to the Lampeter Railway Station proceeding generally in a northerly direction through that parish and in a north-westerly direction through the parishes of Silian of Bettws Bledrws of Llanfihangel-Ystrad of Ciliau-Ayron and of Llanerch-Ayron skirting the parish of Henfynyw and terminating in the parish of Llanddewi-Aberarth in the urban district of Aberayron in a field No. 866 on the 25-inch Ordnance Map of the said parish at or near a point 2 chains or thereabouts measured in a southerly direction from the north-western corner of the said field.

A Railway (No. 2) [being Railway (No. 2) of the application of 1903] 7·3 chains or thereabouts in length wholly situate in the borough and parish of Lampeter commencing by a junction with Railway (No. 1) at or near the southern boundary of an enclosure No. 308A on the 25-inch Ordnance Map of the said parish and terminating by a junction or junctions with the railway or sidings of the Manchester and Milford Railway Company 10 chains or thereabouts northward of the booking office of the Lampeter Station of the said railway:

Provided that notwithstanding anything in this Order contained the Company may with the consent of the Board of Trade make a junction or junctions with the railway or sidings of the said Manchester and Milford Railway Company by agreement with that Company as hereinafter provided at any point on Railway (No. 1) or Railway (No. 2) within the limits of deviation shown on the Plan.

A Railway (No. 3) [being Railway (No. 1) of the application of 1904] 5 miles 2 furlongs 5·25 chains or thereabouts in length commencing by a junction with Railway (No. 1) in the parish of Llanerch-Ayron in the field No. 6 on the 25-inch Ordnance Map of the said parish proceeding generally in a southerly direction to Pen-y-waun thence in a south-westerly direction to Sinefa thence in a north-westerly direction to Oakford thence in a westerly direction crossing the main road from Aberayron to Cardigan about midway between Llwyn-Celyn and Llanarth and terminating in the parish of Llanarth near the westernmost corner of the field No. 3834 on the 25-inch Ordnance Map of the said parish.

APPENDIX

A Railway (No. 4 [being Railway (No. 2) of the application of 1904] 2 miles 5 furlongs or thereabouts in length commencing by a junction with Railway (No. 3) at its termination proceeding in a westerly direction to Gilfach-Rheda thence in a north-westerly direction passing to the South of Llanina proceeding thence in a westerly direction and terminating in the parish and urban district of New Quay at the westernmost end of the field No. 925 on the 25-inch Ordnance Map of the said parish.

12. The railway shall be constructed on a gauge of four feet eight and a-half inches and the motive power shall be steam or such other motive power as the Board of Trade may approve: Provided that nothing in this Order shall authorise the Company to use electrical power as motive power on the railway.

Provisions as to Working

41.—(1) The Company shall not without the previous consent in writing of the Board of Trade use upon the railway any engine carriage or truck bringing a greater weight than fourteen tons upon the rails by any one pair of wheels: Provided that if at any time the rails used shall weigh not less than seventy-five pounds per yard the Company may use upon the railway any engine carriage or truck bringing a weight not greater than sixteen tons upon such rails by any one pair of wheels;

(2) The Company shall not run any train or engine upon the railway at a rate of speed—
(A) exceeding at any time twenty-five miles an hour;
(B) exceeding twenty miles an hour when such train or engine is passing over any gradient steeper than one foot in fifty feet;
(C) exceeding fifteen miles an hour when such train or engine is passing over any gradient steeper than one foot in forty feet;
(D) exceeding ten miles an hour when such train or engine is either passing over any curve the radius of which is less than nine chains or within the distance of three hundred yards from a level crossing over a public road where no gates are erected and maintained across the railway;
(E) exceeding any less maximum speed fixed by the Board of Trade for any part of the railway where the Board consider such further restrictions necessary for public safety.

42. Where the Company carry the railway across any public carriage road on the level the Company shall not unnecessarily allow any train engine carriage or truck to stand across the level crossing.

43. The Company on the one hand and the Manchester and Milford Railway Company or the Great Western Railway Company or the London and North Western Railway Company on the other hand may subject to the provisions of Part III of the Railways Clauses Act 1863 as amended or varied by the Railway and Canal Traffic Acts 1873 and 1888 enter into agreements with respect to the following purposes or any of them; (that is to say)—
   The construction maintenance and management of the railway;
   The use or working of the railway and the conveyance of traffic thereon;
   The regulation interchange collection transmission and delivery of traffic coming from or destined for the undertakings of the contracting companies or any of them;
   The fixing subject to the authorised maximum rates and the collecting payment appropriation and apportionment of the tolls rates charges receipts and revenues levied taken or arising in respect of traffic;
   The supply and maintenance by the working Company under and during the continuance of any such agreement as aforesaid for the working of the railway of rolling stock and plant necessary for the purposes of such agreement;
   The employment of officers and servants for the conveyance and conduct of traffic and all incidental matters.

Appendix Three

Board of Trade Inspector's Report, 1911

RAILWAY DEPARTMENT
BOARD OF TRADE
8, Richmond Terrace,
Whitehall, London SW
12th May, 1911

Sir,
I have the honour to report for the information of the Board of Trade that in compliance with the instructions contained in your Minute of the 26th April, I have inspected the Lampeter and Aberayron Light Railway, constructed under the Light Railway Order of 1906 as amended by the Light Railway Order of 1909.

This railway commences by a junction with the Great Western Railway at Aberayron Junction, near Lampeter, and terminates at Aberayron. It is 12 miles 14 chs. in length, and is a single line, with one passing place at Ystrad, which is just half way.

It has been laid outside the limit of the deviation shown in the plan from 5 miles 3.40 chains to 8 miles 1 chain by agreement with the local landowners.

The width at formation level is 15ft. 6 ins. in cuttings and 17 feet on embankments. The gauge is 4ft 8½ inches.

The rails generally employed are flat bottomed weighing 75 lbs. per yard, and are 32, 26 and 20 feet in length. They are fastened to creosoted sleepers, 9ft by 10 inches by 5 inches, which are laid 3 feet apart and 2 ft. at the joint centres by two ¾" fang bolts at each bearing clip. On some of the curves bullheaded steel rails weighing 80½ lbs. are used, together with 40 lb. chairs, and sleepers 9ft by 9 ins. by 4½ ins. of the G.W.R. pattern.

On one section of the line the bottom ballast consists of G.W.R. slag; on another section of G.W.R. slag and stone ballast; and for the remainder of the distance of stone bottom ballast from cuttings. The top ballast consists of crushed slag or Goodwick stone. The depth below the under side of the sleepers is said to be 1 ft. 1 in.

The fencing consists of posts and wires. No difficulty has been experienced in the drainage.

The sharpest curve on the line has a radius of 12 chains, and the steepest gradient an inclination of 1 in 40. The deepest cutting has a depth of 48.5 feet, and the highest embankment a height of 51 feet.

There are the following stations on the line:-

(1) Ystrad, which is a passing place, and consists of two platforms, 200 feet long, of ample width, and 3 feet above rail level; a waiting room and booking office are provided on the down side.

(2) Aberayron, where there is a single platform, 200 feet long, and 3 feet above rail level, with waiting room, and conveniences for both sexes.

There are the following halts:-

(1) Silian, which consists of a single platform, 120 feet long and 3 feet above rail level, with shelter and ticket office.

(2) Blaenplwyf, consisting of one platform, 60 feet long and 3 feet above rail level; this platform is to be lengthened to 120 feet.

(3) Talsarn, consisting of a single platform, 120 feet long and 3 feet above rail level.

(4) Ciliau, ditto. ditto.

All these stations and halts are provided with name boards and with ample lighting arrangements.

APPENDIX

There are 6 underbridges on the line, of which 5 are constructed with concrete arches and concrete abutments, the maximum span being 25 feet; the other which crosses the River Ayron, consists of steel plate girders with rolled joists, cross girders, and rail bearers, and has a skew span of 59 ft. 7½ inches.

The girders gave moderate deflections under test load of engines, and have sufficient theoretical strength.

There are 7 culverts, of a width varying from 5 feet to 8 feet, formed of concrete, with concrete arches and inverts.

There is one overbridge built of concrete 25 feet span, which has ample clearance.

All these works are very substantially constructed and showed no signs of subsidence.

There are the following signal boxes, viz:-

Aberayron Junction box at the commencement; reported on separately (R.4473).

Ystrad Box, containing 9 levers, all in use, and 2 electric train staff instruments.

Aberayron Box, containing 6 levers, all in use, and a Staff instrument.

There are ground frames at :-

Silian East, containing 2 levers, controlled by the electric train staff of the section.

Silian West, one lever controlled by a special key from the East Ground frame.

Ciliau East, and Ciliau West, each containing one lever, controlled by the electric train staff of the section.

There are a large number of occupation crossings, which are closed in the usual way, with gates opening outwards from the line.

There are 8 public road level crossings, at 7 of which cattle guards with notices on each side, as required by Section 26 of the Light Railway order, have been provided; and at one, viz. public road level crossing, No. 211 on the plan, adjoining Talsarn Halt, gates with targets and lamps have been erected across the railway on each side, as required by section 25 (2) of the Order. With regard to this latter crossing, it was pointed out to me, both by the owning company and the working company, that these gates are a serious disadvantage, as the line on either side is on a very steep gradient, viz. 1 in 41, and unless a man is employed to open and close these gates, before and after the passage of every train, it will be necessary for the train to come to a stand on this steep gradient for the fireman or guard to do so, and in the rising gradient this increases the chances of a breakaway in the case of goods trains. They further pointed out that every passenger train will stop at the halt, that there is a 'Stop' board for all goods trains just before reaching the halt, and that the speed of goods trains coming up the gradient will be very low, so that there is no chance of any train passing the crossing except at very low speed. The road in question is not an important one, and the expense of keeping a man on duty will be considerable, so I can strongly recommend the Board of Trade to permit the removal of the gates at this crossing and the substitution of the usual cattle guards and notices. I do not know if there were any special reasons for having gates at this crossing. The Cardigan County Council are the road authority.

The whole of the work on this line has been carried out in a very substantial manner, and I can recommend the Board of Trade to approve of its being opened for passenger traffic.

I attach an undertaking as to the mode of working, signed by the Chairmen and secretaries of both owning and working companies.

I have, etc.

(Sgd) E. DRUITT
Lt. Col.

Appendix Four

LA&NQLR Chairman's Report, 1913

In presenting the Accounts for the year ending December 30th, 1913, the Directors call attention to the gratifying increase in the gross traffic.

During the past year the negotiations with the Great Western Railway have been continued, and several matters in dispute have been settled.

The construction charge has been settled at £5,128, and the Great Western debenture of £6,305 accordingly reduced to £5,128, leaving £1,177 of Debentures available for issue by the Company.

By an agreement dated July 17th, 1913 the charge of £1,459 7s. 4d. for the first year's maintenance has been withdrawn. So far we have been unable to get the Great Western to reduce their minimum charge of £3,000 per annum for working the line, though the Auto-Car service costs less than the train service contemplated in the working agreement.

The Company received £69 11s. 11d. as Compensation for the reduced service during the strike, and will receive £436 18s. 6d. as surplus on this year's working, after deducting income-tax. The Light Railway has created a good deal of new traffic, - coal, live stock and timber, but owing to the shortness of the line, the greater mileage of this traffic is naturally over Great Western, and not over our line. If the Great Western arrange to carry all the Aberayron mails, most of which now go by mail cart, a considerable extra income would be carried by the Railway.

At present, the New Quay traffic is taken to Llandyssul, a 16 mile journey, occupying two hours in Motor Busses, which do infinite damage to the roads and cost the county and Great Western heavy expense, whereas the traffic could be brought to Aberayron, a distance of seven miles, which would save the County a considerable sum, and help the Railway shortly to pay its shareholders, as both goods and mails would follow the passenger service.

For the first time we are able to place the traffic receipts for two completed years side by side for comparison, and trust that the result will be considered most promising.

I remain, Ladies and Gentlemen,
Your obedient servant,
JOHN C. HARFORD,
(*Chairman*)

Gross Receipts

	January 1st to June 30th, 1912.					January 1st to June 30th, 1913.				
	£	s.	d.	£	s. d.		£	s.	d.	£ s. d.
Passengers	752	19	3			Passengers	893	12	11	
Mails	21	10	0			Mails	21	10	0	
Parcels, etc.,	35	7	4			Parcels	37	19	7	
Goods, etc.,	333	18	4			Goods	431	10	6	
Miscellaneous	2	19	11			Miscellaneous	8	15	2	
Rents collected	8	11	0			Rents	20	18	6	
				1,155	5 0					1,414 6 8

	July 1st to December 31st, 1912.					July 1st to December 31st, 1913.				
	£	s.	d.	£	s. d.		£	s.	d.	£ s. d.
Passengers	1286	7	0			Passengers	1522	12	0	
Mails	21	10	0			Mails	21	10	0	
Parcels, etc.,	57	16	7			Parcels	55	14	1	
Goods, etc.,	446	7	4			Goods	416	18	8	
Miscellaneous	11	1	3			Miscellaneous	18	12	6	
Rents collected	2	19	6			Rents	2	9	6	
				1,843	13 2					2,049 13 1
				2,998	18 2					3,463 19 9

CERTIFICATE AS TO PERMANENT WAY, Etc.

APPENDIX

I hereby certify that the whole of the Company's Permanent Way, Stations, Buildings and other Works, have during the past year been maintained in good working condition and repair.
Lampeter, February 10th, 1914.   S.W. YOCKNEY, *Engineer*

Appendix Five

LA&NQLR Chairman's Report, 1922

LADIES AND GENTLEMEN,-

The Lampeter, Aberayron and New Quay Light Railway was taken over by the Great Western Railway on July 1st, and its existence as a separate Company ceased. Its Board of Directors no longer exists, but as late Chairman of the Company, I am writing a last report on the audited accounts of the Railway's last half-year from January 1st to June 30th, 1922.

The Bank overdraft has been paid off by the Guarantor since the accounts were audited. Beyond the Secretary's salary and the cost of printing these accounts all liabilities have been settled, the office furniture has been sold, the office let, and all books, documents, company's seal, etc., have been handed to the G.W.R.

The payments to the Debenture holders were agreed at 33⅓% of their holdings in Debentures, in 2½% G.W.R. Debenture Stock, as follows:—

	£	s.	d.
Edmund Nuttall	500	0	0
James Nuttall	133	6	8
Gerald G. Lynde	33	6	8
Cardiganshire County Council	4,150	0	0
Aberayron Rural District Council	560	0	0
Aberayron Urban Council	283	6	8
Lampeter Town Council	291	13	4
Lampeter Rural District Council	291	3	4
H.M. Treasury	7,333	6	8
	13,566	13	4

£8,840 was paid by G.W.R. towards the Overdraft of £12,787 19s. 6d. leaving £3,947 19s. 6d. to be found by the Guarantor plus the various expenses of solicitors' costs, etc.

The half-year's traffic receipts did not leave any balance but the G.W.R. paid us the same amount as in 1913 in spite of the bad traffic during this last half-year.

The Directors hope that the Railway will continue to prove a great boon to the district and trust that the advantage of a Railway may compensate for the money lost by the County Council and Local Authorities, and believe most sincerely that the County Council and the Local Authorities will never regret their great share in making this boon, so often talked of and waited for for so many years, a reality which under G.W.R. ownership will they hope produce greater and greater facilities and lessen the burden of road up-keep.

Your obedient Servant,
JOHN C. HARFORD

Falcondale, Nov. 6th, 1922. Late Chairman L. A. & N. Q. Light R.

Appendix Six

Appendix to the Working Timetable, 1939

LAMPETER AND ABERAYRON BRANCH
MOTOR TROLLEY SYSTEM OF MAINTENANCE BETWEEN ABERAYRON
JUNCTION, 0 MILES 4 CHAINS, AND ABERAYRON STATION, 12 MILES 14 CHAINS.

The combined Engineering Gang, whose home station is Felin Fach, is responsible for the section of the Line.

The instructions in connection with the Motor Trolley System of Maintenance on Single Lines worked by Electric Train Token, pages 65 to 68 of the General Appendix to the Rule Book, will apply with the following additions and modifications:-

Places where telephones and key boxes are fitted:-

Group No. 1 (One Key).	m.	c.	Group No. 2 (One Key).	m.	c.
Key Box No. 1	0	4	Felin Fach Signal Box	5	78¾
Key Box No. 2	1	2½	Key Box No. 7	7	5
Key Box No. 3	2	7	Key Box No. 8	8	4
Key Box No. 4	3	0	Key Box No. 9	9	0
Key Box No. 5	4	4	Key Box No. 10	10	8
Key Box No. 6	4	75½	Key Box No. 11	11	3
Felin Fach Signal Box	5	78¾	Aberayron Signal Box	12	8

Note.-The telephones for Group No. 1 communicate with the Signalman at Felin Fach. The telephones for Group No. 2 communicate with the Signalman at Aberayron.

If it is necessary to have occupation without an Occupation Key or Electric Train Token, Handsignalmen must be sent out in accordance with Rules 215 and 217.

Clause 2 of the Standard Instructions will not apply, and the following modification thereof will operate.

Neither the inspection Car, Motor Trolley nor trailer must be placed on the Line, nor must the Line be obstructed in any way, unless and until:-
(a) An Occupation Key has been obtained for the Section concerned, and the Ganger is in possession of it; or
(b) An Electric Token has been withdrawn, and the Ganger has it in custody.
Note (i).-Paragraph (b) does not apply to the Key Box No.1-Felin Fach Section (Group No.1). The Electric Token for the Lampeter-Felin Fach Section must not, in any circumstances, be handed to the Ganger in connection with engineering Department occupations of the Line.
Note (ii).-In the case of failure of the Electric Token Apparatus, the inspection Car or Motor trolley may (EXCEPT IN THE LAMPETER-FELIN FACH SECTION) be used for the purpose of conveying Pilotman (delivering the Pilot Forms) through the Section, or from the point where the Trolley is located, in accordance with Electric Token Block Regulation 25, Clause (c), when, owing to failure of apparatus, an Electric Token of Occupation Key cannot be withdrawn. The Signalman at each end of the Section will be responsible for coming to a clear and proper understanding before the Car or Trolley is placed on the rails, and must record particulars in their Train Registers.

The use of the Inspection Car or Motor Trolley under the provisions of Electric Token Block Regulation 25, Clause (c), is prohibited in the Lampeter-Felin Fach Section.

Should an obstruction occur or the Line become unsafe during any time when the Ganger may be unable to obtain an Occupation Key or Electric Token, the protection required by Rule 217 must be provided, and the circumstances explained to the Signalman by telephone.

Clause 4 of the Standard Instructions.

The switch must be turned to the 'In' position before turning the ringing key of the telephone. The telephone switch must be tuned to 'Out' position before the Ganger leaves the Key Box.

APPENDIX

Clause 11 of the Standard Instructions.

The following to be added:-

Before going off duty each night the Ganger must arrange to place the Occupation Keys in the Key Boxes at Felin Fach, and before leaving duty each night the Signalman at Felin Fach must withdraw the Occupation Keys from Groups Nos. 1 and 2 respectively. The Occupation Keys must be locked in the Box fixed outside the Signal Box Door. The Ganger is supplied with a key to the Box, to enable him to obtain the Occupation Keys therefrom before the Signalman is on duty. The Occupation Keys must be inserted in the Key Boxes in the respective Groups ten minutes before the first Train is due to leave the Token station at either end of the Section; the Signalman being informed by telephone when this has been done.

When the Signalman at Felin Fach comes on duty in the morning, he must satisfy himself whether the Ganger has taken the Occupation Keys from the locked box, and if the Ganger has not removed the keys, the Signalman must replace them in the Key Instruments.

SIDING ACCOMMODATION.

Traffic in full wagon loads can be dealt with at Silian Halt, Felin Fach Station, Ciliau-Aeron Halt and Aberayron Station, and the Siding accommodation at these places:-

Silian Halt	6 wagons.
Felin Fach	30 wagons.
Ciliau-Aeron Halt	12 wagons.
Aberayron	45 wagons.

SILIAN HALT SIDING.

This Siding is connected with the Running Line facing from the direction of Aberayron, the points being worked from a Ground Frame locked by the Electric Train Staff.

The Line is on a gradient of 1 in 78, falling towards Lampeter, and the greatest care must be exercised by the Guard in performing the work at the Siding. Before the Engine is detached, the Train must be secured by the brake van being applied, also a sufficient number of wagon brakes, and if necessary make use of sprags on the rear wagons next to the brake van, in accordance with Rule 151, to prevent the Train or any part of it moving.

The Siding will be worked by Down Trains as required and will accommodate 6 wagons.

The Guard will be responsible for working the Ground Frame points, in accordance with Electric Train Token Regulation 34.

FELIN FACH STATION AND CILIAU-AERON HALT.

Wagons can be put off and picked up by Up and Down Trains as required.

ENGINE WORKING.

The Engines authorised to run over this line are the 0-4-2T A, B, C, H and M 48XX and 4-4-0 A13, for Passenger traffic, and 0-6-0T L, N and O, and 0-6-0T A.38 for Goods Traffic.

WORKING OF BALLAST TRAINS.

Ballast trains formed of not more than six wagons and Brake Van may, when necessary, be propelled from Lampeter on to the Aberayron Branch, provided that the leading vehicle is not permitted to pass beyond the summit of the 1 in 48 gradient near Blaenplwyf Halt between 2 and 3 m.p.

In all such cases the leading vehicle must be a Brake Van, in which the Guard must ride, keep a sharp look-out, and be prepared to warn anyone on the Line.

The instructions on page 20 of the General Appendix to the Rule Book, and Rule 149-exception (vii), must be observed.

Bibliography

'The Lampeter-Aberayron Railway', *GWR Magazine*, December 1908
West Wales - The New Railway; Through the Aeron Valley to the coast by GWR, GWR promotional booklet, 1911
'The Lampeter and Aberayron Railway', Alfred W. Arthurton, *Railway Magazine* Vol.34, p.333, 1914
'The Lampeter, Aberayron and New Quay Light Railway', J. Bourne, *Trains Illustrated*, August 1953, p.312
Aberayron Transport, Lewis Cozens, privately published, 1957
The Manchester & Milford Railway, J.S. Holden, Oakwood Press, 1979
New Quay and Llanarth, W.J. Lewis, 1981
The Vale of Rheidol Light Railway, C.C. Green, Wild Swan, 1986
Farmers & Figureheads, S.C. Passmore, Dyfed County Council, Carmarthen, 1992
'The Aberayron Branch', W.H. Smith & C. Turner, *British Railway Journal* No. 16, 1995, p.662.

Acknowledgements

The National Archives, Kew
The National Library of Wales, Aberystwyth
The Ceredigion Museum, Aberystwyth
The Welsh Industrial & Maritime Museum, Cardiff
New Quay Public Library
The Narrow Gauge Railway Society
The Industrial Railway Society
Champlain Protex Ltd, Felin Fach
The Bodleian Library, Oxford

N. Bird, M.N. Bland, R.E. Bowen, G. Briwnant-Jones, R.M. Casserley, C. Chapman, P.F. Claughton, M. Cook, T. David, F.K. Davies, D.G. Geldard, G.W. Hall, Mrs M. Harrison, J. de Havilland, B. Hilton, J.S. Holden, G.B. Jones, R.P. Jones, Revd R.W.A. Jones, R.W. Kidner, Mrs A. Lloyd, Dr J.D. Owen, Mrs V. Palmer, R.L. Pittard, I. Pope, R.N. Redman, J.E. Shelbourn, P. Walton.

In 1988 the 'Aeron Express' over Aberayron harbour was revived. This view from the south side of the harbour shows the carriage crossing towards the north side, 26th July, 1989. Unfortunately this enterprising attraction fell foul of health and safety legislation and closed in 1994. *Author*